# AMERICANS
# ARE ALONE
# IN THE WORLD

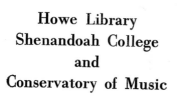

# LUIGI BARZINI

# AMERICANS ARE ALONE IN THE WORLD

**THE LIBRARY PRESS**

**New York**

1972

# Reflections 1972

THERE ARE, OF COURSE, many reasons why you could profitably read today one of yesterday's travel books. It may be a rare historic testimonial (Marco Polo or Hector St. John de Crèvecoeur); wildly inaccurate but entertaining (any of Alexander Dumas' fanciful accounts of his voyages); the memorable reflection of a great mind (Goethe's *Italienische Reise*); or the pathetic panorama of a vanished age, as fascinating as an album of old snapshots. Some contain uproariously wrong or frighteningly accurate valuations and prophecies (Custine and de Tocqueville).

This slight book of mine may perhaps deserve attention for an entirely different motive. To be sure, I'm far from being as distinguished as the above mentioned authors. I was a diligent, cautious, and experienced journalist, always checked facts and the spelling of proper names, but at a certain point in life, began to suspect that truth might often be more easily revealed by frivolous details, random remarks, casual anecdotes, the conversation of obscure strangers, than by momentous events, historic documents, solemn speeches, or the vacuous and slick statements of public personages.

The book is therefore based on trivial notes, taken at one of the revelatory moments of American life, the early fifties, when the people's traditional and undisturbed concepts of themselves, their country, their ideals, and their mission in the world were being tested and slowly modified by the agonizing duties imposed on them by history. Most Americans were not clearly aware of what all this would cost them in the future, and neither, of course, was I; they were proud, brave, and ready, but also vaguely troubled and unhappy. In retrospect we now know those years, like the early thirties, were at the same time the sunset of an era of comfortable illusions and the dawn of a new anguished age.

I was in a unique position. I had the opportunity of revisiting the United States after an absence of about thirteen years. Absence notoriously sharpens the eye, brings out the tiniest changes in dear and familiar faces, and often reveals taken-for-granted details as disturbingly significant.

The face of the United States was dear and familiar to me. Perhaps I know the country better than some Americans, too busy to pay attention to what is really going on about them, and than most foreigners, whose knowledge is usually based on hurried trips, American books, films, magazines, and newspapers. Foreigners seldom realize that most American sources are contaminated by an emotional urge to demonstrate one thing or another, to console or delude the author as well as the reader, to prove America still is, never was, surely will be soon, or will never be one thing or another. Bitterness or disappointment often makes Americans assert the opposite of what they wish to be true, in the hope of being convincingly confuted.

I liked to think I knew better than that. I had been a student in New York for five years in the 1920s; my first sweetheart had been American; some, perhaps most, of my old friends were American (Americans have a reckless capacity for friendship that cautious Europeans lack). I had crossed the continent a couple of times, in both directions, in broken down old cars, then known as jalopies. I worked one summer as a cub reporter on the *New York World;* another year I got myself a job on the *Flushing* (Long Island) *Evening Journal.* Flushing was then still a little country town, at the edge of New York, with a monument to the Civil War soldier, a street dedicated to the Union, a court house with pillars, a red-brick armory, an ancient Quaker meeting house, and immense trees that bathed everything in trembling green shadow. It was on the side of a long creek which ended in vast, grey, stinking garbage dumps.

The publisher who hired me, Mr. Clemens, was rumored to be a relative of Mark Twain, possibly a nephew. He was an old, bald, pale-faced man with watery eyes who spoke with a Southern drawl. He wore a green eyeshade over his glasses, elastics on his shirt sleeves, a bow tie, and suspenders. His roll-top desk was out front, by the street entrance, behind the show windows (on which the Gothic letters of the masthead were written in gold), by the side of the low wooden swinging door, near Betty, the telephone girl, reception-ist and secretary. His was a strategic position. He could watch the street, spy who came in and out and at what time, and, through the open door, what went on in the editorial room.

Mr. Clemens looked me over (I was an eager nineteen-year-old boy) and described my duties. I was to be a police reporter at seven a.m.; a copy reader and headline writer later in the morning; an assistant makeup editor around noon; and a feature writer in the afternoon, to prepare copy for the next day's inside pages that would keep the linotype operators busy. "And, of course," he added, casually, "you'll pitch in when necessary and help the other men in their work." (This proved to be one of my most time-consuming tasks. The three other men often got drunk on bootleg booze and I, who did not drink, had not only to carry their burden but also sometimes carry them home.) For all this I was to get fifteen dollars a week. I was glad, of course, for the opportunity to make that much money but more for the chance to improve my English prose and enrich my professional experience in so many directions all at the same time.

Mr. Clemens then looked closely at my name and address. His face showed astonishment:

"Luigi?" he asked. "Are you Italian?"

I admitted it. "And can you read and write?" he asked incredulously. I reassured him. I could read and write well enough for the *Flushing* (Long Island) *Evening Journal.*

I left the United States in 1930, after graduation. There was clearly no future for me in America at that time. As a matter of fact, there was no future for almost anybody. The Depression was on its way; the unemployed were already selling apples on the streets and lining up in front of soup kitchens. I returned to Italy, got a job in the *Corriere della Sera* in Milan, slowly worked my way up from local stories to international events of secondary interest, until, one day, in 1933, I was dispatched to the United States for a *reportage* on the New Deal.

Three years later I was assigned to cover the 1936 election campaign (I got a splendid interview from Alf Landon in Kansas), and three years later still, in 1939, I was sent back to appraise the mood of the country "on the eve of the war." The temptation to stay behind was almost irresistible. However I felt it my duty to return to Italy, got back just before Hitler attacked Poland, was assigned to London that winter, eventually ended up in a Roman jail, in the spring, for political reasons, and a few weeks later was assigned to forced residence in the boondocks.

The war, the underground work, the immediate postwar turmoils, family problems, the uncertainties of the future, the difficult reconstruction of my life and the country's prevented my leaving. I worked hard, edited dailies and magazines, and ran for office. Finally, in 1952, I felt I could go without feeling I was deserting. Things had become relatively stable, as much as they could be in Italy anyway. I went back to the United States.

To be sure, many things had changed in America in the meantime. It would have been surprising and frightening if everything were as I had left it, as immutable as the *New York Times* typography or the smell of American french-fried potatoes. Some of these novelties the reader will find described in the following pages. The most obvious — those which my New York friends, old schoolmates, married girlfriends, and colleagues, were particularly proud of and never tired of pointing out — were more or less what I expected.

Glorious old landmarks had disappeared, of course; new buildings had been raised to unprecedented heights; more bold new bridges spanned rivers in all directions; new fashions, new tunes, new dances were the rage; new slang expressions were incomprehensible to me as the old familiar ones had become incomprehensible to the very young; young ladies used words young ladies had never used before, in public anyway.

All this — and the fact that many people I knew had died, vanished, without forwarding addresses, changed husband, wife, profession, political party, *Weltanschauung*, diet, name, home, and in a few cases, religion too — I considered drearily normal. More interesting and puzzling were less conspicuous changes which took me a few days to become aware of and longer still to define. They were undoubtedly the visible signs that a social revolution had taken place in the 1930s and the most expensive war in history had been fought and won a few years before.

To be sure, the social revolution had already been embalmed by specialists and could be studied in history books (in the United States history has always followed the newspapers by a short neck). It had left its unmistakable mark in laws, rhetoric, prejudices, editorials, school textbooks, the brooding silences of the lovers of *temporis acti*, the bold ideas of the intelligentsia, and everyday conversation. My feeling (possibly erroneous) was that the revolution had not been as deep as some believed or feared. It had not apparently disturbed the fundamental creeds and what Americans thought was their national character and the purpose of life.

I had to admit, however, that the very rich were not as fashionable as they had been in the past. They were no longer openly and innocently admired, envied, forgiven for their feats, marital adventures, sins, and extravagances. Their philanthropy had increased (or the publicity surrounding it; it was difficult for a foreigner to distinguish which), as if it now had become the principal justification for wealth. They were no longer the models for the humbler to imitate. Their medieval castles, *Petits Trianons*, Renaissance *palazzi*, stately

English homes in the country, or *hotels particuliers* in town were often inhabited by decrepit survivors of another era, surrounded by decrepit retainers, or sold to nunneries, boarding schools, and commercial establishments.

An old friend of my father, a retired banker whom I visited in Long Island, no longer lived in his vast English manor, rich with armor, tapestries, and old masters, at the center of an immense park. He had retired to a little flat in the neighboring village and visited his princely home during the day. He told me he could find and pay enough servants and gardeners to keep it as a museum but not to live in it. Maybe also the moral burden of acting the role of a Medici and living far above the other people had become too uncomfortable.

The American saga of the self-made man, who was born on a farm, delivered newspapers in his youth, became an honest laborer with callused hands, went to night school, and turned into a benevolent plutocrat with white piping on his waistcoat, was no longer a regular feature of magazines and Sunday supplements. Great private balls were no longer respectfully described in the society pages, with all the details of the decorations (ballrooms transformed into Persian gardens, Versailles salons, or tropical gardens with flowers flown from the Caribees) and long lists of guests.

All this was particularly disturbing to a European journalist. European correspondents had tirelessly described the life of the American rich, the "king" of this or that commodity, and of American outlaws (the

Western and mobster varieties), for almost a century. It was what the editor, and presumably readers too, wanted. The gangsters were still there, but not the rich. What had become of the American dream? Immigrants had been lured to the United States not by a life of drudgery and exploitation in the slums, on the railroads, or in the mines, but by the hope of becoming (or seeing their sons become) millionaires, legally if possible.

The natives themselves often went through misery, years of dreary work, docile obedience, and hardships in heartless and efficient industrial organizations with the same wonderful hope in their hearts. "One day our ship will come in," said penniless husbands embracing bedraggled wives in the movies, and both their faces reflected the light of the radiant future. Natives, immigrants, as well as men who had not left their native countries, consoled themselves reading about millionaire heroes, the Great Gatsbys, just as the Greeks of old had listened to tales of prodigious mythological characters or medieval peasants of knights, magic incantations, fairy godmothers and lower-class toads turned into upper-class princes.

The questions raised in my mind by all this were difficult to answer. Had America really been as obsessed with wealth in the past as foreign observers and the American popular press led us to believe? My private recollections were inconclusive. All my friends in the university wanted to make money, lots of money, of course. So did I. But none of us wanted to sacrifice the pleasures and satisfactions of life to the boring, stupid, and dehumanizing sport of amassing greenbacks. My friends and I, however, were probably not typical. Most of us were horrified by business careers and fascinated by books. We wanted to write.

One must remember that Americans, like the Chinese, when observed long enough separately at close quarters, no longer look alike. In fact they vary greatly, more than many other people, each one dissimilar from all his countrymen. When you get to know a few really well (which means when they stop talking to you as to a foreigner) most of them reveal themselves to be, more or less like all human beings, pathetic and brave, baffled, to be sure, by their own unique and terrifying contemporary problems, but tortured also by the eternal problems.

And yet, dissimilar as they all are, Blacks, Whites, Jews, Gentiles, Mediterraneans, Northerners, or Asiatics, there is something elusive which makes them all unmistakably American and makes it easy always to spot them in a foreign crowd. This is not only clothes, voices and accents, because a trained eye distinguishes them even silent, in disguise, in bathing suits, and sometimes naked. It must be (this is only an hypothesis) the outward reflection on their faces and bodies of their American ideas. The fact that Americans are not as uniform as the superficial observer thinks makes it almost impossible, for anybody who knows them at all well, to generalize convincingly and to write plausibly about them.

Was, for example, this shift away from wealth which I noticed after the war a local phenomenon due to the American social revolution of the 1930s, or was it also a sign of the times, common to most of the Western world? Everywhere or almost everywhere the elite had tried to shed the visible trappings of privilege, royal princes rode bicycles and sometimes married stenographers, millionaires dressed and behaved like working men, famous personages tried to disappear in the crowd, wore sunglasses, and lived in the shadows.

Had society really changed as much as people thought, and could it really change in a country where the majority had always belonged (or believed they belonged) to the middle class anyway? The revolution had undoubtedly been a middle-class revolution, had consolidated middle-class ways, ideals, advantages, privileges; it was only natural that everybody, as it happens after all revolutions, outwardly adopted the style of the winner, the new ruling class. But had not many of the American rich always been uncomfortable in their princely role, had they not always been ready to play poker in their shirt sleeves in some back room and to exchange jokes with old friends?

There were other, more subtle changes, which I found difficult at first to define and explain. The typical American seemed to me to have grown stouter, flabbier, and curiously facetious. The tweedy, lean, pipe-smoking characters I had considered common — maybe I had noticed them more because they flattered a preconceived idea of mine, maybe they had really been common in college lecture rooms or newspapers' editorial offices — seemed to have become scarce. Their habitual pose had been a kind of jovial grumpiness, their humor pointedly disagreeable. Perhaps they were afraid to be taken for servile toadies, as they had always been afraid to seem unmanly. Men never carried a cane, seldom wore spats, and never a monocle, sure signs of un-American effeminacy. They said gruffly: "You look like a decaying corpse this morning," "You won't last long," "I hope you choke." "Drop dead," "Get lost," "I hope you get run over by a streetcar," and "What's your poison?"

Now (in the early 1950s) the prevalent pose was one of forced cordiality, as if they wanted everybody to think they were *simpatico* and to love them. The idea that Americans wanted to be loved at all cost at this point in their history was puzzling and distressing. Why? They made flattering remarks. They told me I was a remarkable man, I amazingly spoke English with no foreign accent (which is not true), reassured me that I looked young for my age and in the very best of health. This friendliness seemed at times slightly more than strictly necessary, including that of New York doormen and shop clerks, who, as a rule, had always been proudly rude and contemptuous in the past.

People I had just met now called me by my first name, and not only fatherly gentlemen like Mr. Clemens who, years before, sometimes did so with a paternal air, but also men younger than I; and all insisted I call them

Tom, Dick, or Harry in return. "Why does Luigi always call me *Maestro* or Mr. Rogers?" complained Richard R. Rogers to a common friend. "Doesn't he like me?" I liked him, of course, but had not known him long and felt I had to show respect for his fame and age. I would have been mad to call Stravinsky "Igor" or "Igor Fedorovich." Had I ever called Arturo Toscanini, a friend of the family, anything but *Maestro?* (Even his wife Carla called him Toscanini, or "Tosca" for short.)

Moreover, my dark Italian appearance and accent no longer provoked the disdainful responses (or the pointed courtesies) of old. Could Americans have changed so much that they no longer considered a Mediterranean origin an unpardonable aberration, but a vaguely amusing and perhaps even a charming and enviable advantage? Was all this in some way, also connected with the bitterness of increased competition among them, which deprived them of the old-fashioned pleasure of making unnecessary enemies? Was it somehow related to the fact that they were not as lean as I remembered them? Did they no longer despise good food as something to be enjoyed occasionally, but fundamentally heathen, good only for the Chinese, the French, the Jews, the Armenians, and the Italians?

Did they no longer go in as assiduously for Spartan sports? Had their blissful certainties been weakened by the Depression? Could the Depression and the war have taught many of them understanding, tolerance, and respect, if not appreciation, for foreign ways? Could it be that the people who had defeated the greatest economic slump and won the greatest military conflict in history had acquired doubts about their superiority in the very moment of their triumph, when they had emerged as the *Numero Uno* of all Empires and the richest in history?

Gradually I began to suspect Americans, at least some of them, were no longer as greedy for hard work nor as keen on efficiency as they had appeared to be. Work had not been for them (I was thinking of Mr. Clemens) Adam's curse but life's fulfillment and a real pleasure. When I dropped into friends' offices, during my first trip after the war, I saw them beam with delight not only at my visit but at the interruption. They no longer expressed polite regrets (between telephone calls) not to be able to chat with me as much as they would have liked; they no longer asked briskly, "What can I do for you?" They now said: "Good to see you, have a drink, do you smoke cigars, what's new?" put their feet on the desk, told their secretaries not to put through any calls, and seemed relieved at the chance to stop working. Some went out for lunch for and hour or two, like Romans or Parisians. More and more of them were not in the office on Friday.

All this troubled me. I had always envied the Americans' capacity to sit whole days at their desks without so much as lifting their heads to look out of the window. Was this a significant change? How significant and how much of a change? Had, to begin with, Americans (I mean the single human Americans I new and not Americans unconsciously impersonating Americans in front of a foreigner) been really as greedy for hard work, discipline, and efficiency as they had appeared to be? Had the high income tax, as I had been told, robbed them of the pleasure of making money? Were they secretly rebelling against their iron fate?

Was the Calvinist ethic weakening? One could not tell from figures: the GNP was rising all the time. Perhaps they had discovered that hard work was not always the best way to increase production and to make money, let alone solve difficult problems. Did the phenomenon appear more significant because of my age and my friends'? It was only natural that young men in their twenties pedalled harder to get to the top of the rise and mature men in their forties allowed themselves to coast downhill when possible. Older men (like older sportsmen) learn to avoid unnecessary efforts. I could not reach a convincing conclusion.

What interested me perhaps more than anything else were the few things which, in a society dedicated to perennial change, in which change was life and immobility was death, remained imperturbably identical, as the isolated rocks overrun by breakers reappear from the swirling foams glistening and streaming with water, but intact and at the same place. Obviously, I concluded, the first few days, after my first arrival in the early 1950s, as I walked about, overheard people's talk, looked at the immutable water tanks on the buildings' roofs, at shop windows and people's faces, sniffed the smells and listened to the noises, rode subway cars, New York was unmistakably still New York. To be sure, the subway cars were dirtier than I remembered them (the whole city was dirtier as well) and gone was the handsome gold-lettered warning that a *500-Dollar Fine* awaited anybody who spat on the floor (maybe the warning had become ineffective because nobody spat or because nobody was any longer intimidated by mere typography). Still they were substantially the subway cars of my youth. They smelled the same and made the same noise.

This sensation that not everything had changed comforted and reassured me on my very first morning. Like all air travellers from Europe, I woke up at dawn, long before room service could supply me with a cup of coffee. I dressed and walked a few blocks to an all-night luncheonette, where I sat with unshaved and sleepy taxi drivers, truck drivers, a crummy old woman, a drunk, some clean-looking boys and girls who had had a good night's sleep and a good wash, and a policeman. Some of the customers were holding the *Daily News* in front of their faces. The huge cryptic front-page monosyllabic headline screamed something about an arrested murderer, *"COPS NAB BOB."*

The smells were familiar and unmistakable: American coffee, bacon, french fries, scalded grease on the hot plate, eggs. As always the waiter kept on drawing coffee from the spigot and pouring it back into the top of the glistening machine. (Only Americans do that. Other peoples have discovered that keeping coffee hot by boiling it over again gives it a dark color but also an acid

and metallic taste.) The signs on the mirror behind his
back, advertising the day's specials; the customers'
voices, their honest New York accent, the weak and
worn-out wisecracks repeated without a smile, out of
one corner of the mouth; the waiter's orders shouted to
the cook, his reassuring answers to customers
("scrambled eggs coming up"), his conjurers gestures,
the hiss of the machines; and then the taste of the hot
watery coffee, of the salted butter on the toasted insipid
bread ... I felt as if I had never been away, was
twenty-five years younger with a pink police-card under
the ribbon of my fedora.

I discovered later, during that first visit (and later
again, when, for one reason or another, I had to return
more and more often, until I found myself somewhere
in the United States almost once a year), that many
more things had never changed — and probably would
not change in the future, or change only on the surface
— than *News* headlines, beaneries' food, and their
customers' looks and manners. (Even in this field, to be
absolutely honest, a few things were different. Almost
gone were the old wagons on the vacant lots, the honest
sign *EATS,* and some of the roughest proletarian
"specials.")

As the years went by, I unwillingly seemed to be
gathering a mental collection of some of these perennial
qualities of American life, but could talk about them
with only a few American friends. (Most of the others
were politely shocked at my insistence that a few things
that mattered went on almost unaltered from one gener-

ation to another, and thought me a foreign screwball
with a European *idée fixe*.) These random observations
irritated me too. I relegated them to the attic of my
mind as unusable, while I went about my real business,
which was meeting important people, reading fresh documents, reports, speeches, newspapers, books, attending
press conferences, and picking the brains of other journalists, in order to gather material for my articles.
Articles are supposed to be as brilliant and short-lived as
fireworks. Like them, they must illuminate the contemporary scene for a fleeting moment. Journalism, I had
been taught at Columbia, is the recording of the new,
the bizarre, the timely, the different; it must avoid the
immutable, permanent, longer lasting than bronze.
These constant traits in American life were obviously
unusable; some were uninteresting and insignificant,
anyway, but a few were possibly revealing clues.

One of these — and I write about it in the following
pages — was practically unchanged since my college days
( and surely for more than a century-and-a-half before).
It was the firm and enviable belief, shared apparently by
most Americans, the simple, the sophisticated, and the
anticonformists too, that all life's riddles had answers at
the end of the book, as they can be found in honest
textbooks of mathematics and in well-constructed
detective stories. This was and remains a most reassuring
belief. Time, Americans thought (and many of them
probably still think), was a gentleman, did not cheat,
and would eventually take care of everything; somewhere surely there always is a still unknown young man

(or a team of them) making revolutionary inventions, discovering new miracle drugs, formulating a new scientific law, devising a machine, working out the answers. He did not always have to be a genius, like Leonardo da Vinci. More often he was just "one of us."

Incidentally, this seems to be another constant trait. For some reason, Americans like to think that Great Men are like everybody else and prove it by saying that "they put their pants on one leg at a time." This necessity to appear to be "one of us" at all costs makes astronauts talk like schoolchildren on a picnic, prevents eminent scientists, scholars, thinkers, heroes, or statesmen of today (not of the past) from delivering immortal lines. Deep emotions or high thoughts often are expressed in the form of weak jokes. The press always reports these quotations eagerly, to confirm the myth that "all men are more or less the same" and that practically anybody could write the Faulkner opus, discover the structure of DNA, or write a great symphony, if only he had the proper equipment and took the time.

Any "one of us" knows what one has to do when facing a problem, any problem, a personal affair, a family difficulty, a financial decision, a scientific enigma, but more particularly the Big Problems which Great Experts or the President's staff have to work out. One must not lose one's head. One indiscriminately gathers all the data, mountains of data, the more the better; gets the best minds together; collects money, the more money the better; chooses the best leader; works out a new formula, a novel approach, and, almost inevitably, invents new ingenious contraptions; finally sets up a suitable organization. Then one waits, like the gardener who has properly prepared the soil and placed the right seed in it, for something to sprout. This is how the Panama Canal was dug, yellow fever defeated, and the atomic bomb built. Significantly enough, among these guiding rules one was usually missing or given little weight — the study of precedents, the lessons of history, possibly because the past was believed to be generally misleading and hope was only in the future anyway. ("If only President Johnson had read *De Bello Gallico* he would have avoided many mistakes ... " an old European observer of American life complained to me many years later.)

If results are slow to appear, all one had to do was double the ante, increase the efforts, the work, the funds available, the number and expertise of experts, the length of conferences, the size and complexity of the organization, the amount and thickness of reports, and, if necessary, perfect the machine or machines invented for the purpose or devise new ones. Naturally, Americans are at times uproariously wrong. Not all difficulties can be exorcised that way. At times the machinery becomes so cumbersome and labyrinthine that it stops working altogether, making complicated problems completely insoluble. But the irritating thing is that Americans obtain results often enough to be confirmed in their unshakable faith, and to make fools of the wise, skeptical, doubting, cautious, ancient Europeans. Americans are able to untangle tricky knots, with brilliant new approaches, often enough to dazzle foreigners and to show the way to the rest of the world. It may even be, sometimes, the wrong way.

This belief made Americans immensely strong; nothing on earth and beyond seemed to be impossible to them; they appeared to dispose of most barriers. But, at the same time, it made them morally more pathetically vulnerable, thin-skinned, embittered, and defenseless than other people. It is at the origin of their perpetual discontent, their restlessness, the *angst* which tortures them, their secret lives of quiet desperation. They are perpetually resentful and impatient. Why, they seem to ask, when a solution surely exists and can be found, do we put up with such discomforts, injustices, and ills? Why has it not yet been found?

The fact is they cannot easily endure failure or defeat. Europeans and others are often grateful that some nostrum of sorts has assuaged some of their ancient ills, that things are not as bad as they could be, and they look no further. Americans are forever disappointed that the definitive answer has not been discovered (they refuse to believe that sometimes there is no definitive answer, or there could be many competing unsatisfactory ones), that things are not as good as they could be, and that some of the successful remedies sometimes provoke worse miseries than those they cure. What many Americans find particularly incomprehensible is that while the method usually (but not always) works wonders in scientific research and the application of technological knowledge to practical ends, it does not seem to be thaumaturgic in other fields.

People asked (and still ask) you, at dinner, on television, or in the more thoughtful magazines, the same question: Why don't we spend as much to solve problem *A* (a cure for cancer, the integration of the blacks, world peace, the decay of cities, the corruption of social life, *la condition humaine,* or the revival of vanishing moral values) as we do in sending men and gadgets into space? The answer, of course, is that Americans have been conditioned by their past to do things in a tidy manner, according to the book, *a regola d'arte,* to face with greater ease problems for which the answers are measurable, calculable, verifiable, certain. They are so comfortable with this way of disposing of difficulties that they try to stretch all problems (even those which tortured ancient Greek philosophers or medieval theologians) on the Procrustes' bed of mathematics.

This tendency may be characteristic of the middle class all over the world, or it may be due to a native repugnance for abstract thinking. The Americans' preference for pragmatism, science, and numbers may make them wary of the lure of abstract thinking, which gives one the illusory feeling of having coped with the matter, and of all theorizing which cannot be confirmed by means of experiment. This may also be one of the visible signs of their compulsive urge (possibly a national trait) to control hazards, defeat blind chance, forestall the mysterious workings of Fate, guide Divine Provi-

dence, abhor exceptions and irregularities, dominate the
stormy and contradictory confusion of life and nature.
This is curious to observe in a people who believe they
had crossed the ocean and filled a continent in the
pursuit of risk and adventures, as well as for the fearless
love of the very hazards they work so hard to abolish.

This contradiction, of course, may not be uniquely
American but part of the essential nature of all men,
who often try to destroy the very things they most
desire. Lawless Italians are among the keenest scholars
of jurisprudence, and boast of being the inventors and
teachers of Law to the world; great gamblers search in
vain for a system to break the bank at Monte Carlo and
to abolish that very delicious uncertainty which keeps
them at the green tables day and night and fills their
empty lives. Who else would have dedicated so much
energy, crusading enthusiasm, money, political sagacity,
and legislative ingenuity to the abolition of alcoholic
beverages than Americans, who drink and possibly need
the consolations of hard liquor more than any other
people (with the possible exception of the Russians)?

On my first visit in the early 1950s, the United States
was hesitatingly but proudly trying out its role as the
World's Greatest Imperial Power of All Times. The role
was undoubtedly new, but, like other American
novelties, not as new as many were inclined to believe,
nor was it really as unwanted and unexpected. It is true,
of course, that Americans had always been tempted to
ignore other people's squabbles, isolate themselves,

cultivate their own fertile garden, and mind their own business, which, as Calvin Coolidge authoritatively pointed out, was business.

It is also true that (as Lord Bryce explained long before the Spanish-American War and the liberation of the Philippine Islands) "they have a well-grounded aversion to the incorporation or control of any community not anxious to be one with them," perhaps because "their administrative posts set up in a dependent country would certainly be jobbed, and the dependent country itself probably maladministered," as a result of which "all such work (in the past) has been badly done and has given rise to scandals."

On the other hand, it is well known that some kind of irresistible imperial streak had been evident from the beginning, a philanthropic urge to spread the blessings of American ways, which include good sanitation, the rule of law, commerce, parsimony, and technology as the mother of affluence; to feel responsible for the welfare and happiness of different, heathen, and distant people; to defend them from the greed of Europeans or their own lack of foresight and prudence; to help them to become what Americans believe to be every man's desire, a tolerable imitation of the American model; and to exercise a jealous and very emotional defense of American interests, anywhere in the world.

These two tendencies have not proved to be as contradictory as they might seem. At no time have Americans tolerated foreign interference in their own country and continent (they made this perfectly clear in a number of circumstances and in several fundamental documents) but, at the same time, always felt incapable of standing by and letting what they considered distressing developments occur almost anywhere, to the south or across the two oceans. The list of their military expeditions abroad is a long and familiar one. They intervened decisively in Mexico, China, the Philippines, Cuba, Nicaragua, Panama, and elsewhere. They waged two world wars in faraway places.

To be sure, the Korean conflict (which was being fought when I returned to New York) had not been secretly plotted in Washington by greedy imperialists, or enthusiastic do-gooders. It had been crudely forced on a pacific United States by ill-informed and naive, if exceedingly well armed, aggressors. It, too, had inevitably awakened the old American proud certainty that no enemy (least of all a poor, underdeveloped, illiterate and enslaved enemy) could stand up for long against the impact of the American native virtues, the real source of American power.

These enviable virtues are the wartime version of peacetime virtues. They include the capacity to work together in immense numbers towards one clear goal; to share the same, simple, fundamental ideas; to fight bravely and to die for them; nimbly to create organizations *ad hoc* as unexpected needs arise; to disband them when no longer useful; to let mistakes and defeats suggest improvements and corrections; to design all the necessary new gear, vehicles, planes, and diabolical weapons; to mobilize immense material and technological resources in order to produce and transport hardware and supplies quickly and in great quantities.

The war once again also brought out that great American military traditional knack, irritating to all European strategic experts, including Karl Marx, of preferring dreary massive logistics to brilliant Napoleonic maneuvers, and, in the end, preferring the dull but thorough general, George Brinton McClellan rather than dashing Philip Sheridan, Dwight Eisenhower rather than George Patton. Among the American wartime assets is also the honest repulsion to "the incorporation or control" of conquered lands, which reassures allies, enemies, and the Americans themselves; as well as the compulsion to feed the hungry, clothe the naked, cure the sick, among the conquered people as well as their own. It all makes defeat by Americans tolerable and sometimes even desirable.

Things, notoriously, did not entirely turn out in Korea — and later in Vietnam — according to the prescribed pattern. For the first time in history, the American virtues proved themselves inadequate. The primitive enemy was not as impressed as he should have been by the display of terrifying science fiction machines and techniques. In fact, the very presence on the battlefield of such expensive and contrived weapons and vehicles tended at times to weaken the American soldier's will to fight. Had he not been taught since childhood that the machines would always do the trick and were irresistible in war as they had become indispensable in peace? Not only were the primitive enemies not frightened but they also fought on valiantly with whatever cheap and old-fashioned and homemade arms they possessed. They occasionally won victories and managed to neutralize the splendid and expensive effort of the Americans, simply because their men did not mind dying in droves, in the obsolete way of the Spartans at the Thermopylae.

All this, at the time of the Korean War, was new and disturbing, particularly because the situation, as friends saw it and explained it to me, looked unmistakably simple, as simple as similar situations had seemed in the past. The Good Guys were, as always, on one side ("our" side), and the Bad Guys on the other; the Good Guys were defending justice and fighting for liberty and progress; the Bad Guys were the aggressors (nobody could deny it), ill-fed, ill-housed and regimented slaves resigned to their own servile condition and conscripted to make all men slaves. Why should there have been any doubts about the outcome? Didn't the Good always win? Furthermore, wasn't God (or History) on the side of the big reinforced batallions, especially if they were also well fed and well armed, and backed by a disciplined, moral, intelligent, industrious, highly organized, technically efficient people, enlightened by science, animated by lofty ideals, and strengthened by the most nearly perfect political institutions ever devised by man? Had the United States ever lost a war?

The fact that the armies in Korea suffered at times costly reverses, embarassingly often in front of television cameras, and had to fall back in disorder to what the military euphemistically call prearranged defensive lines was considered at the time grievously unfortunate but normal. Such things had always happened to victorious armies. Americans had known bloody but temporary defeats in their most fortunate campaigns. The setbacks in Korea were usually compensated, anyway, by subsequent victories and the occupation of vast expanses of territory.

What really began to worry and bother some Americans in those years was the fact that, for the first time, there seemed to be no way to convince the enemy once and for all they had been beaten and had no choice but to sue for peace. That the Americans would not lose in the end was taken for granted, but nobody seemed to know how they could win. *This* sort of thing had never quite happened before. Defeated enemies must always recognize their defeat. Not these. More and more Chinese and North Koreans came in waves to be slaughtered, as if their reserves were inexhaustible, and their lives meaningless. Nothing seemed to slow down or stop the flow.

Many explanations were offered, that life counted for nothing to people enslaved by a totalitarian tyranny; the Good Guys always won but nobody could tell how long it might take; the enemy leaders were too ignorant and fanatical to know they had no chance; the Soviet Union found it convenient to keep the war going, weakening China and the United States; some American commanders had, unfortunately, made a number of grievous mistakes; timid politicians in Washington were thwarting the brilliant conceptions of the generals which would have ended the war in a matter of weeks or months.

Only a few began to suspect that the system which had produced wonders in the past, both at home and abroad, in peace and war, no longer worked automatically in the contemporary world under all conditions. What had gone wrong, the system or the world?

I went to see George who had come back from Korea a few weeks before. He had been at Columbia University with me. Born in Oregon from a New England family, he was blond, blue-eyed, tall, muscular, vigorous, optimistic. In the old days he had loved racing cars and girls. Once in a while he disappeared for days to go on what was called "a binge." This was to me an esoteric American ritual of sorts, a kind of self-punishment, a period of exile from reality comparable to Eleusinian mysteries or the retreat good Catholics go into when in the spiritual dumps.

When he reappeared he looked disheveled, incredibly dirty, with bloodshot eyes, black-lined finger nails, a few days' growth of golden stubble, dirt-filled wrinkles, and little crusts on his face. He then went to the local gym and worked hard for a few hours, emerging in the end wonderfully healthy, clean, and in excellent humor. How he (and many others like him) did it, I do not pretend to know. It was a miraculous American gift. A "binge" would have destroyed me for weeks.

George had been a test pilot for experimental planes

in the early '30s, joined the Marine Corps air force, rose in rank, married a petite blond wife, Amy. Then he left the service, entered a Wall Street firm of sorts, bought a house in Connecticut at the edge of a wild wood, and raised hemp-blond children. He had fought the Japanese in the Pacific and, when the Korean War broke out, had been recalled to the service.

George and I had absolutely nothing in common. When sitting on speakeasy bar-stools, in the old days, one next to the other, I sometimes looked in the fly-specked mirror behind the bartender at the two twenty-year-old boys, and wondered what made us such good friends (we still are) — one relatively small, black-haired, black-eyed, with a shrewd and cautious old man's expression on his pale face, and the pink and happy giant exuding sanguine certainties.

Perhaps each of us was seeking solace from his own hereditary virtues. I thought George was the United States, the reckless and irreverent new wisdom of the Republic, the magic know-how, the indestructible health, the vigorous and fearless life. I vaguely imagined that, somehow, once I had comprehended George, America could have no secrets for me. What he saw in me I can only guess. He was possibly mystified and fascinated by my addiction to books, the odd bits of useless information that issued from me unexpectedly, the foreignness, the ancient Mediterranean world (upon which his teachers had for some pedantic reason taught him to look with awe). Who knows?

Amy was preparing dinner for us while we had drinks.

She was tireless and cheerful. She had a very full day: breakfast for everybody, work in the garden and in the house (which had included, that day, the painting of six doors), supper for the children, dinner for us. Once again I had to take notice of one of the subtle differences between the American Empire and all those which had preceded it, possibly a precious clue of sorts, which, if properly interpreted, could possibly lead to some significant conclusion.

The more the national power, wealth, prestige, and responsibilities increased, the more American women of all classes (even many who could afford not to) went back to the backbreaking work of their great grand-mothers, the early settlers, the pioneers. Amy, in another age and another Empire, would have lived in a sumptuous marble mansion, not in a tiny imitation colonial wooden house; and, reclining languidly in expensive clothes, she would have directed an army of slaves or servants to do all the jobs she was gaily doing herself.

George, of course, was enthusiastic about his Korean experience. He had seen the war from behind desks or from the air, and this had saved him from some of the more gruesome daily experiences of infantrymen. He told funny and pathetic anecdotes, described the stunning new planes, the gadgetry devised since the previous war, the technical advances in all fields, and the stupendous machines that were still in the experimental stage. He called the North Koreans "gooks" without venom, as if that was one of their proper names. He had no doubts that Providence had been generous to the American people giving them a man like General Douglas MacArthur at the time of need.

"Mac," he said, "is the best man for the job since Caesar. He's a great statesman, a great leader of men, a great strategist, as well as a great fighter in action." But the politicans in Washington had him hamstrung. He wanted to end the war, i.e. to do the things that would win it, invade Manchuria, blockade the China coast, unleash Chiang Kai-shek. Each of these moves, to be sure, was risky and could have provoked unforeseen reactions.

"But," George said, "when decisions are taken boldly and fearlessly, the execution is quick and resolute — you have superiority in the air and at sea — you choose the spot and the time to strike — the enemy is always taken by surprise, dominated psychologically, forced to surrender ... This is the way we have always done it."

After dinner, George sadly admitted that perhaps MacArthur with all his gifts had been born at the wrong time in history. Maybe the politicians had something. There was a real danger that the Soviet Union, which could not afford to see China humiliated, would start an atomic war, "WW III"; or that the United States would get itself bogged down in an infantry war in China, a nightmare. How many millions of men and how many billions of dollars would it swallow, decade after decade, without hope? And would the Americans stand for being bled white of all their wealth and their best youth? He also admitted that the NATO allies had some reason to be worried.

"Wars," George said, looking intently at the ashes of his cigar, "used to be simple. You fought as best you could and you won. It was always the other guy who lost. Some guy died, some guy came back alive, and you forgot the whole thing. But why should war still be simple when life itself is getting more damned complicated every day? I'm not the type who looks for traitors in Washington. There may be some, of course. There have always been in all our wars. But they never really decide the outcome. There are other reasons for our failure."

"The problem," he went on, as if talking to himself, "is that in the world of today an honest, old-fashioned man is hobbled — an honest country is not free any more to do whatever is necessary to bring a war to an end, a war it never wanted anyway. Nobody understands us and what makes us move any more. Why do even our friends accuse us of ulterior motives, diabolical schemes, imperialistic aims, aggression, when all we ask is to help others and come home and get on with other jobs? You know us, Luigi. You know how simple we are, how honorable our intentions, how disinterested, and how incapable of intrigues, deceit, skulduggery . . ."

Later, as I came and went, as the defense of the United States worldwide involvements and responsibilities, as well as the preservation of its power and influence, became more and more complex and irksome and the cost practically unendurable, the imperial role began to pall on many Americans. They discovered with aggrieved surprise that not everybody was ready to accept the authority of the policeman pounding his beat, not everybody took for granted his right, capacity, and will to inflict punishments on all transgressors. There was a real danger that the United States would eventually end up like the cop played by Charlie Chaplin in *"Easy Street,"* on whom kitchen stoves and garbage rained from first-floor windows.

In other words, not every inhabitant of the rest of the world (as well as some Americans) completely and wholeheartedly shared the Americans' officially proclaimed conceptions, trusted their motivations, and entertained all of their traditional hopes. Even such ideals as economic development or peace, which any sane man would be tempted to consider universal, i.e. shared by all men in all stages of sociological development in all parts of the terraqueous globe, turned out not to be quite everybody's dream.

There actually seemed to be people on earth who preferred the joys of slaughtering their enemies (and accepted a life of unendurable sacrifices to do it) to the tranquil pursuits of industry, agriculture and commerce, people to whom war, hunger, and death seemed more desirable than the life they led. All this, of course, should not have come as a surprise. A careful reading of American history would have shown that many Americans, including Southerners and the aborigines, at one time or another, had preferred war and death to making the economy blossom.

To be sure, by the early 1950s many American leaders had learned that not every man, European, East Indian, Chinese, Korean, as well as American Indian or black descendent of Southern slaves, wanted to transform himself into the American model. (Only a few years before, Roosevelt still believed this or pretended to believe it. He used to say that all that was necessary to destroy Communism in the Soviet Union was for the United States Air Force to air-drop enough Russian copies of the Sears Roebuck catalogue . . .)

Yet the majority of leaders (perhaps all of them) could not openly and officially abandon the belief that, in some way, all human beings — and not only the West and East Europeans, but also nomadic Bedouins, Kalmuks, naked inhabitants of tropical jungles or fur-clad Eskimos — who, for reasons of their own, might not want to become imitation Americans, were, nevertheless, *au fond*, fundamentally, *mutatis mutandis*, more or less as the Americans imagine themselves to be, and that they would react as Americans are supposed to in front of any given situation, for they were people who could be reasoned with, who could be persuaded, who were amenable to the dictates of "common sense," and left to themselves, they would ultimately choose the right road.

Here, of course, I should interrupt this introduction with a few remarks with which to try to define what

Americans mean when they say "American" or "typical American." While the word is often applied to all the inhabitants of the United States indiscriminately, it has numerous other overlapping connotations. It somehow now stands for "the kind of person produced by an advanced industrial civilization, a man mainly conditioned by the rules necessary for orderly mass production and consumption" (as in: "The Japanese are becoming more and more like Americans").

At other times, the term seems instead to describe a particular specimen, a middle-class, patriotic, hardworking man, living predominantly in the tidy suburbs of the Northeastern states and the Middle West (more rarely also in other parts of the country), a man still shaped (positively or negatively) by the Puritan inheritance, inspired by noble Eighteenth-Century ideas, who firmly believes, among other things, in a better future. More rarely, but significantly, the word is loosely employed as the good contrary of the bad "un-American." In this case, one should define "un-American" first, to know what "American" means, an almost impossible job.

Americans cannot easily abandon their deeply rooted conviction that every human being on earth is fundamentally like what they conceive or hope themselves to be because, to be sure, it has some foundations in reality, but also because it is not an ordinary presumption but an article of faith, in fact, the very foundation of the Republic. The Republic rests notoriously on the certainty that not only the Americans, but every man, everywhere on the planet, today as in the remote past and the future, is endowed with common human qualities, among which is innate and natural goodness; that he knows how to distinguish good from evil and would avoid evil; and that there is no limit to his perfectibility.

There are, of course, as there have always been, as many exceptions (some of them monstrous) as confirmations to this imaginary law of Nature, exceptions of which Americans have always been well aware. Being pragmatic and respectful of the facts of life, they have successfully coped with them for centuries, within their own continental frontiers and in their foreign relations. This is the reason they passed immigration laws, built jails, and put policemen and soldiers on the payroll. But they always managed, one way or another, to explain away all deviations from the ideal norm. They cannot do otherwise. They cannot officially and publicly give up this article of faith because, if they did, they would no longer be American. They would lose their *raison d'être* and their moral strength; they would become as weak as Antaeus when no longer in contact with Mother Earth.

Let the reader not be mistaken. I, too, think that it would be wondrous if all men were good and, in moments of intellectual weakness, I even manage to believe it: if everybody behaved decently, problems would be simple and life more acceptable. I, too, tend to be persuaded that the American ideals represent the most advanced point reached by Western man in political thinking. Having lived under one totalitarian dictatorship and visited several more modern models, I also believe that the American experiment (or some of its imitations) with all its bugs, corruption and ineptitude, its senatorial rhetoric and back-alley violence, is the only workable form of government not only for men who want to be free but for all men because it is endowed with self-adjusting mechanisms which rigid regimes lack; that most of what appear to be grave contradictions on the American scene often are, in reality, but the struggle of bodies and antibodies in a healthy and developing organism.

Nevertheless, I also regretfully have to admit that the generous application to the world of American rules of conduct and beliefs did not solve all problems. Sometimes it even made them more complicated. As could already be seen in the 1950s, the Americans, deluded by their abstract conception of the nature of man and by their staunch optimism (which can often be a subterfuge of the timid to avoid disagreeable decisions), stumbled open-eyed into visible traps.

It has always been known (and American leaders sadly admit it behind closed doors, and off the record) that it is almost impossible to gain political ends without a little unpleasantness. Politics, especially international power-politics, is not a bowl of cherries. It has been known for centuries that, in order to enforce peace or to make war, one must prudently start from a pessimistic conception of the nature of man, singly and in the mass, and presume he can be maneuvered when necessary by guile and force, toward what the leaders hold to be his own good. Man, of course, singly or in the mass, is not always the poor creature of the pessimists. One must, however, consider such cases as encouraging exceptions.

The cynical approach is obviously much more difficult in countries where democratic liberties are preserved and the people are well informed, than in countries where the elite is not worried by scruples, civil liberties are unknown, or, at best, a make-believe façade. The sense of anger and outrage among free citizens when they discover the double deals behind the scene, the real reasons which appear to inspire fateful decisions, particularly when they may have led to stalemate or defeat or catastrophe, can be as overpowering as a tropical hurricane and sweep everything before it. This is especially so in societies where the people are still committed to, or conditioned by, a moral or religious tradition.

It is almost impossible to hide forever from the citizenry the deceptions, ruses, machinations, subterfuges, and simple lies which, unfortunately, appear to be necessary, even in the best of democracies, to carry out an honorable policy with some hope of success. Abraham Lincoln pointed this out once, that one "could not fool all the people all the time," but implicitly admitted that short-term or partial deceptions were, if not acceptable, sometimes conceivable. Surely he had learned one could not always conduct a victorious war without them.

Many causes for the Americans' disappointing performance, disappointing to themselves above all, were already evident in the early '50s. Perhaps the goals were too ambitious, and inevitably so. Innate American apathy in international affairs tends always to be overcome by hysterical and hyperbolic rhetoric. Perhaps they had overestimated their own power, the patience and fortitude of their own people, and the terror their tools and tactics could inspire. Above all, they had gravely underestimated the envy, hostility, suspicion, fear, and misunderstanding all their moves could provoke. Furthermore, the fact that the times were abnormally fluid, troubled, and confused had not been taken into sufficient consideration.

Mad and irrational ideologies threatened world peace; simple expedients which had once been safely employed could not be depended on for long; plans had to be revised continually; technical advances transformed the strategic value of faraway places; some clusters of allied nations which the State Department had worked hard to put together might well have to be loosened or even dissolved. As the missiles could travel farther and farther with their deadly charges, more and more airbases all over the world became useless and the agreements with the local governments (usually expensively paid for) obsolete.

Then, of course, contemporary circumstances were so

different from those faced by the Empires which had imposed their particular peace on the world in the past that precedents could seldom be used as guides — always supposing that Americans in the 1950s were inclined, or had the time, to learn from history. One of the few "cold wars" between East and West one could study in the past had been that between the Christian West and the Moslem East. Historical analogies are notoriously deceptive, but perhaps this much could have been learned from this ideological confrontation: it lasted for centuries; neither faith conquered the other in the end; whoever dominates the Mediterranean controls the European mainland (something the Romans and the English had also known); ideological confrontations often conceal other and less visible causes of rivalry; and Christian princes (including the king of France, the Republic of Venice, or the Pope himself) did not disdain allying themselves to the Sultan against their Christian brothers, from time to time, whenever it suited their interests. . . .

Previous Empires have been able to rely on their overwhelming military superiority over more primitive enemies. The Persians had their cavalry, the Macedonians the phalanx, the Romans their wall-like legions, the Spaniards dominated their possessions with the unbeatable *Tercios*, the English and the Venetians cultivated naval power. The Americans, too, possessed an overwhelming superiority for a few brief years, the most overwhelming superiority of all times, but it was somehow impossible for them to make use of it. They were paralyzed, aside from immediate circumstances or sagacious calculations, by their humane and moral inheritance. This also prevented them from using their superiority as a threat to gain diplomatic advantages; nobody believed they were capable of using the frightening new weapons, if the bluff were called, against any enemy who had not yet developed the same kind of explosive.

Previous Empires have been able to move freely and practically unobserved in a world without laws. They waged distant wars without the consent or approval of their own subjects, or any concern about international public opinion. Fleets at sea and armies on the field were not followed by swarms of critical and incredulous journalists and TV camera crews. Weaker enemies could be massacred or disreputable secret agreements concluded with no other worry than the possible verdict of future historians. Americans, on the other hand, were always forced to move gingerly, on tiptoe, looking to right and left, consulting everybody, allies and neutrals and opponents, observing as much as possible the decencies of international law and the Queensberry rules of war. Awkward diplomatic lies were soon found out, their innermost state secrets revealed to the world. It was proven time and again that it was against their very nature (in Lord Bryce's phrase) "to enslave people, to occupy territory," as it would be to drag defeated enemy chieftains in chains behind a conqueror's chariot down Pennsylvania Avenue. How else could one terminate wars and dominate the world? Could new ways be explored? Would they be successful?

In addition to all the historic and moral reasons which I have hurriedly sketched above (and there are many more) which made the United States unable to procure, once and for all time, for itself and all others, the beneficial effects of empire, and "everlasting *Pax Americana*" guaranteed by international law, there is another reason which I believe is worthy of notice. Americans were obligated almost overnight to tackle perhaps the most arduous problem in history: how to have the heroic pride of a guiltless conscience, be applauded and loved by everybody, and, at the same time, preserve the order of a world hegemony and do the occasionally nasty things necessary to enforce the law. Or, as the Italians say, how to "have a full barrel and a drunken wife."

Machiavelli pointed out long ago that this was not quite feasible. He argued that Christian morality did not hold in political affairs, and that any policy really based on the assumption (not the pretension) that it did, would end in disaster. Perhaps the Americans had not had the time to discover the practical impossibility of performing the task to their entire satisfaction without offending their official ideals. The burden had been dumped in their lap, practically without warning, at the end of the war, for no other reason than there was nobody else around. Wasn't the United States the most powerful and successful nation in the world? Didn't it want peace? Then it had better get busy.

The dangers were so great, evident, and frightening, the new responsibilities so obviously unavoidable, that there was no opportunity for hesitation or yet another round of the historic debate between isolationists and interventionists. When Truman intervened in Iran and Greece and said, "I believe that it must be the policy of the United States to support free people who are resisting attempted subjugation by armed minorities . . . We shall not realize our objectives unless we are willing to help people to maintain their free institutions," nobody was surprised. Nobody could read the appalling future implications concealed behind those excellent words. They simply seemed to confirm what everybody knew, believed, and accepted.

Nobody could realize at the time that the very origin of the Americans' power had not necessarily prepared them for its inevitable consequences. It had not taught them to conceive realistic worldwide strategic plans, or the art of making friends and influencing foreign peoples, of preserving peace (as the English had done) by always supporting the Number Two against the Number One, of dominating (as the Mafia sometimes successfully manages to do) without actually using force. The power of the United States ultimately came — as I point out in the following pages of this book — from an extraneous and irrelevant virtue, a knack it had developed in less than one hundred years, something which it excelled in and taught the world: the capacity to produce endless quantities of identical objects at low cost, to improve their design and efficacy untiringly, to transport them to wherever they happened to be needed.

The new responsibilities imposed (as the wars had done before) the rapid mobilization of vast cadres, sometimes to be put to the test in a matter of weeks. This did not seem difficult, at the time, in a country which always believed good inexperienced men can take charge overnight of complex mechanisms and make them work successfully. It had taken previous Empires a century or two in order gradually to reach their apex, and it was time amply sufficient to cultivate the capable and prudent men, generals, admirals, proconsuls, merchants, diplomats, financiers, linguists, historians, jurists, politicians, ethnologists, and philosophers, who established precedents, made the errors, suffered the defeats, won the victories, and in the end developed the techniques necessary to cajole, seduce, intimidate, paralyze, placate, blackmail, defend, and sometimes educate and enrich dependent people.

The Americans could rely only on a single generation with a few brilliant and skilled men. In the 1940s and '50s they had to make do with specialists in other fields (mainly the men who had studied, nursed and administered the growth of economic power, scientists, managers and professors) to advise politicians and determine profound policy lines. All of these experts had to tackle unprecedented problems *in vacuo*, abstractly, from zero. They had few guiding rules. They were compelled to play the whole thing by ear. They shut themselves up in think-tanks, like part-time Trappists in their cloisters. They developed new approaches, sometimes in a great hurry, to prevent the possible spread of epidemics, the outbreak of revolutions, or World War III. There was no other way. The job had to be done. The complex and ponderous jargon or the starry-eyed optimism with which these improvised consultants sometimes couched their concepts seldom concealed the fact that they were baffled and, sometimes, frightened.

Unfortunately, the best scientists, managers, and professors, in the United States as well as anywhere else, often reveal themselves surprisingly inept, more inept than ordinary intelligent nonspecialists, when dumped on unfamiliar ground, to take on problems outside their competence. They fall easy victims to false analogies. They are tempted to oversimplify and distort complex embroglios to make them seem understandable, principally in the hope of placating their own anxiety, sometimes translating everything into some sort of mathematical formula which could be digested by computers. They tend to perceive mainly the facts that confirm their prejudices or desires, often to rely on ready-made omnibus *en-tout-cas* schemata.

They naturally tend to dismiss confusing, irritating, irreconcilable, and unexplainable contradictions as irrelevant. They prefer to think of men as one sees them from tall buildings, uniform insects, or as aseptic statistics, rather than the sometimes erratic, pathetic, and inexplicable beings they reveal themselves when seen at close quarters. Above all, scientists, managers, and professors are accustomed to the sheltered laboratory, the fixed schedule, the well-defended office, the cloistered library, the tidy reports, the controlled conditions and the obsequious aides. They lack the humble skills of men who have to work with lackadaisical unpredictable nature, the skills so to speak, of sailors, fishermen, farmers, horse tamers, the people who must at all cost avoid deceiving themselves and must develop prudence, patience, skepticism, resignation, as well as great fortitude and perseverance.

These are, of course, the qualities which statesmen must have or must acquire, as the materials they handle are not physical objects but natural phenomena. It is not by chance that the leaders of the Roman Republic and the men who built the British Empire had deep roots in country life. Similarly, most American Founding Fathers were the sons of farmers, sailors, or merchants, men fully aware of and prepared for the wanton ways of reality.

Incidentally, most of the American Fathers as well as the British (and naturally the Roman) leaders were familiar with Latin and Greek, imbued with the classical spirit, and knew how to trim sails to the winds of history and keep a watch for sudden storms. Our contemporary experts, particularly American, mostly brought up in contact with machinery, are tempted to believe — or to hope — that, once the proper coin is inserted in the proper slot, and the proper button pushed, the proper effect will follow. This makes them unreasonably despondent and desperate when the results are not what they expect from the premises and the calculations.

To all these limitations one must add a few typically American traits, common to academic specialists, clever technocrats, as well as the common people. They all believe (or struggle hard not to believe, at times) that treaties, written on good paper, signed by the right dignitaries, stamped, sealed, ratified, and exchanged, can be solid bulwarks against the unpredictable; that international bodies created by treaty can be unyielding dikes against the floods of history; that peace, in the end, would be better defended anywhere on earth by the good will of the people themselves, led by their legally elected leaders, than by craft, subterfuges, intimidation, blackmail, or massive armaments; that once men got to know each other better (by exchanging students, tourists, teachers, by sending politicians with their wives to visit their counterparts), they would discover there were few real differences between them, would come to fundamental agreements, consolidate the peace, and love one another.

There is a mysterious riddle in all this, a contradiction foreigners seldom suspect exists and almost never study. Americans in the 1950s did not worry about it and shrugged their shoulders when it was mentioned. Why should the United States have been so severely paralyzed (and is still often hampered), in the efficient and ruthless handling of international affairs, by its optimism *à tout prix,* its prejudices and preconceptions, mostly of a moral character, when these did not always interfere with the solution of internal problems? In other words, why did the same men behave soberly in their private lives, in business, and national affairs, as if they knew that reality was seldom what they wished it were, while they often were so disastrously trustful abroad?

Foreigners tend to conclude wrongly that Americans are naive. They point out any number of well known and undeniable facts. How often were Americans caught out by events? How many United States ambassadors have encouraged or determined the victory of a despicable and dangerous tyrant whom they believed to be a simple agrarian reformer or the Father of his Country, a local George Washington? How often has the State Department put its trust in an inviolable treaty, only to be surprised and chagrined when it was violated? How often have Americans been offended by the anti-American policy of a country which had been fed, developed, and made prosperous with American money? Why did they try to ignore the fact that there is no such thing as political gratitude and that one cannot buy friendship?

The myth that Americans have been and are incurably innocent, at all times and in all their endeavors, can be easily exploded. The United States is also the home of the Philadelphia lawyer, the horse trader, the real estate developer, the second-hand car dealer, the professional gambler, the wooden nutmeg. Among the things

Americans invented or improved is the poker game, financial shenanigans, the art of stock exchange speculation, the rackets, and all those ingenious petty swindles which are known in Italy as *truffe all'americana.*

Surely, few traces of naivete or excessive trustfulness are to be found in American life. Secrecy, which is officially considered wicked (although necessary at times) in the conduct of foreign policy, has always been amply resorted to. Treaties signed with Indian tribes were seldom considered inviolable and sacred. Americans know that next-door neighbors who speak the same language and see each other all the time can hate each others' guts much more than people who speak different languages, live far apart, and seldom glimpse each other. Americans also know the good will of elected politicians cannot be trusted very far. No President in my memory was ever considered a *chevalier sans peur et sans reproche,* a great and farseeing statesman by everybody, at least while he was alive. Every one of them was carefully watched at all times, by a suspicious press.

It can also be proved that Americans did not always lack finesse in international affairs either, particularly when their vital interests were at stake. In 1797 a mission in Paris defeated the wily intrigues of Talleyrand (surely the most astute of all statesmen); Louisiana was bought from the French and Alaska from the Russians at bargain prices by the Americans who shrewdly exploited favorable political opportunities; the separation of Panama from Colombia was engineered with Bismarckian vigor by Theodore Roosevelt. Even the handling of international problems after World War II was not always or solely directed by starry-eyed idealism. In fact, a few of the American errors were provoked not by candid simplicity but by enthusiastic experimenting with crafty, Machiavellian schemes, as in the case of the Bay of Pigs or the backing of unnatural and ruinous political coalitions in foreign countries.

In spite of what critics say, both in the United States and in Europe, the American performance after World War II must be considered a success. It can be called a failure only in contrast with the excessive utopian hopes raised and the vast amounts of money spent. The nature of man has not been changed, to be sure, and the world is still an unhealthy and dangerous place in which to raise a family. Nevertheless, the big ultimate war, which many believed to be imminent and inevitable in the late 1940s and '50s, has not broken out; the earth has not been pulverized by nuclear explosions; humanity has not been reduced to a handful of ragged survivors; the few little wars which erupted here and there were isolated and sometimes smothered before they had grown dangerous; the Korean War was brought to an unsatisfactory but honorable end. At the same time, industry and international trade flourished practically everywhere; the primitive economy of backwater countries began laboriously to develop; colonial empires collapsed; the standard of living of almost every inhabitant of the globe has risen; prosperity, as it always does, has provoked social unrest but has prevented revolutions.

How much of all this was the result of the American planning and perseverance, the intelligence and foresight of its politicians, generals, and think-tank seers, and the product of mathematical formulas digested by computers? Diligent journalists could easily prove (and have often proved) all these theses by digging out the proper documents, facts, and testimonies. How much was success, on the other hand, the quite unintended and inevitable consequence of the country's disproportionate weight, wealth, and power? How much was it the product of historic forces or, as one's grandfathers used to say, the working of Providence? Is there some truth in the old saw, as in all saws, that God protects babies, drunks, and the United States?

It can be said that the *Pax Americana* arises from all these causes and many more besides, possibly from the same complex origins as the U.S.A.'s economic and military triumphs. All victories are the product of the collective behavior of men facing crises, the test of their acceptance of their common ideals, the proof of the cohesion of society. The *Pax Americana,* likewise, can be considered the result, artless, artful, or both, of the Americans' own virtues, beliefs, and ancient hopes (or their conceptions of these things), including their eagerness to tackle problems to improve the world, and their deep assumption of being right. Success was helped, perhaps, by the very reluctance or lack of enthusiasm with which the people at times accepted their burden, a reluctance which made them cautious, willing to experiment, diffident of precedents, advice, and the lessons of history. On the other hand, it was made difficult by the traditional pragmatism of Americans, the trial-and-error method, which makes them confront events as they happen but seldom allows them to foresee what is coming; and their belief in "common sense" which helped baffle them whenever history showed itself immune to it. Henry Luce once impatiently told me in Rome: "I'm sick and tired of Italian problems. They can all be solved with a little common sense." Why nobody in Italy applied common sense to problems was, of course, the real problem which escaped him.

The job was terrifying. The penalty for failure was hair-raising. How could one secure imperial results without becoming an Empire (in the traditional sense of the word) and remain uncontaminated by imperial vices? How could one secure peace without betraying one's honorable principles (or betraying them as rarely as possible)? How could one do all this while keeping the country on its course toward the vaunted future? How could one solve the world's problems without neglecting one's own; how spend all that money without bankrupting the economy? How could one secure cohesion and discipline while preserving the basic liberties of Americans?

Americans have struggled hard, disinterestedly, expensively, through grievous mistakes, failures, and catastrophes. They have slowly discovered that peace cannot be secured once and for all but must be defended daily, that treaties are *chiffons de papier,* and that it is not true that all men are like what Americans imagine themselves to be, but that they, the Americans, are unfortunately like all other men, frail and sinful, and condemned to Man's predicament.

L. B.

*Rome,*
*July 1972*

# AMERICANS ARE ALONE IN THE WORLD

# I

*Sail, sail thy best, ship of Democracy, of value is thy freight, 'tis not the Present only, the Past is also stored in thee.*                                    WALT WHITMAN

"WAR OR PEACE?" ask Americans of the newly landed European. "War or peace?" asked the friend with whom I had a drink my first day in New York, the minister from Baltimore on the train between New York and Washington, the State Department official I had known many years. "War or peace?" asked Bert Andrews, Pulitzer prize winner, head of the *Herald Tribune* Washington Bureau, lifting his eyes from his paper-littered desk.

It was an embarrassing question. Nobody apparently wanted to know if I had read some secret document or if I had stumbled across authentic news of the Kremlin's designs. What they expected me to know, I think, was what European chanceries were doing, what was on their minds—as if European chanceries were busy shaping history. I was being treated like the emissary of the obscure powers who alone determined the future. "How long will Europe allow us to live in peace?" they seemed to ask. They appeared anxious for an authoritative answer, which would either reassure them or fill them with anguish.

In other words, they expected the very same answer we Europeans go to America to seek.

Out of timidity, modesty, humility, inertia, nostalgia or habit, they ignored the fact that we, in Europe, know little and decide nothing. They never admitted the fact that they, the Americans, are alone in the world and carry war and peace on their lap, and that nobody can advise, help or guide them. They seemed to cherish the illusion that the common peace is watched over by the Home Fleet, the Etat Major, the Deuxième Bureau, the Intelligence Service, the Grosse Generalstab, the Foreign Office, the Quai d'Orsay, and Palazzo Chigi, perhaps because in all those majestic offices there still sit grave and imposing gentlemen to whom one can write letters, from whom one can receive learned reports, and whom one can visit.

As a newly rich villager sometimes pays the debts of the ruined duke and keeps him in luxurious style in order to be invited to dinner and dream that he is still living in another world, so perhaps Americans finance and prop up all those venerable European institutions so that they can be comforted by the feeling that they are not alone, that these are still the good old days when others, across the sea, studied the great problems and took the fateful decisions, while they, the Americans, went about their own business. Of course, the illusion is never perfect. Sometimes the newly rich remembers that it is his money which keeps the castle brightly lit and the Americans realize that it is their power, their prudence, and their will which keep the free world together, but they do so only rarely and reluctantly.

Peace or war? I tried my best to answer the perennial question. I said Peace or I said War, according to whom I was talking with, the mood, or the day, demonstrating both conclusions with rigorous historical arguments: for peace, that only a balance of forces had in the past preserved peace and that today the balance had been reached, if not the arithmetical balance of men and weapons, at least the balance of fear; for war, that never in history had two great rival alliances faced each other without, in the end, fighting a war. Meanwhile I sought the real answer in America, traveling everywhere, visiting military and cultural establishments, talking with experts, officials, colleagues, unknown traveling companions, officers, politicians.

Undoubtedly the answer is to be found in the mysterious mechanism which determines political decisions (and the course of history) in the United States, a mechanism which baffles all Europeans, who attempt vainly to attribute to American politics the same conscious motives which have guided their statesmen for centuries. The mistake is common both to the friends and the enemies of the United States: the friends crediting the Pentagon and the State Department with long range, Machiavellian plans, the enemies seeing in all American decisions the cynical desire to dominate and exploit the world. The friends say, "The Americans knew what they were doing when they first withdrew their troops from

Korea." The enemies say, "What the Americans want in Korea is mineral resources and a market for their products."

The European mistake is understandable; the laws which govern the actions of men and the course of events are notoriously the same, in the long run, for the past and the present, in Europe and in America. It is, however, extremely difficult to discern them clearly at work in the confusion and the contradictions of American life. What uniform rule can reconcile the sudden collapse of the American armed forces after the war, the distribution of surplus weapons to friends and enemies, the timidity when confronted with Russian arrogance, the loss of China with the bewildering about-face, the Truman Doctrine, the Marshall Plan, the quixotic engagements, the boasting, the immense military budgets, so large that even American industry could not absorb them? How can one reconcile the strict tariff policy of the United States with the earnest work and the billions spent in order to persuade the nations of the world to trade freely?

Nevertheless, the answer is there, in the very contradictions of American life, in its elasticity, in the rapid violence with which danger is recognized and faced, in the rejection of precedents, in the ready acceptance of new situations. "Americans learn very quickly," a British Labour M.P. said to me some time ago, after a trip to Washington, "but they always start far behind." Europeans are therefore forced to observe the labor of American statesmen somewhat in the way that decrepit Alpine

guides, in the village square, might follow through a tele-
scope the progress of a group of young, willing, bold
and inexperienced climbers on the smooth face of the
mountain. The veterans know the dangers, the illusions,
the false roads, and could point out the tried short cuts
and the shortest route, but their voices cannot reach the
mountainside. They must sit and wait until the young
men gain the experience known to generations, learn
the right way and reach the summit.

In the last few years, for instance, Americans have
discovered—at their and our expense—the advantages of
secrecy, after for more than a century having considered
a cards-on-the-table diplomacy to be a cure for most of
the world's ills; they have found, too, the useful mechan-
ics of the balance of power. Wilson's Number One Point
was "Open covenants openly arrived at" and his supple-
mentary Points spoke of the abolition of all "leagues and
alliances," "special covenants," and of "the great game,
now forever discredited, of the balance of power." The
Yalta conference, according to Franklin Roosevelt, was
to be "the end of the system of unilateral action and exclusive alliances and spheres of influence and balance of
power and all the other expedients that have been tried
for centuries and have always failed." Americans have
now discovered that armaments are an umbrella which
should be used not only when it rains, but which can be,
according to popular belief, handy at all times, because
it often has the magic power to prevent rain from falling;
that right without might is nothing; that a nation must
trim its international ambitions, however noble and

humanitarian, to its actual present power. Europeans now foresee that, in the near future, the United States will be obliged to discover the technique of *divide et impera*, which will naturally be called some strange new name and justified according to up-to-date theories.

Americans are neither naive nor ignorant. The very rules which they ignore and have to discover in the conduct of international affairs have always governed the conduct of their private affairs, the struggles between rival groups, political battles, and the competition of great industries. Something, however, has prevented them from applying their everyday knowledge of human nature and of the use of power to the international field. It is this noble reluctance which baffles and sometimes frightens Europeans. They do not understand it. They do not know that there is a fundamental, irreconcilable contradiction in American political thinking, older than the Declaration of Independence and the Constitution, as old as modern man. The United States is a nation founded in the rebellion against the ancient order, a nation which cherishes a new wisdom, and which is at the same time an ancient Christian nation attached to traditional moral values. It is revolutionary and conservative, like the Daughters of its Revolution, the inventor of the system to break the bank and the owner of the casino, cops and robbers at the same time.

Only rarely, reluctantly, secretly and, driven by fear, may Americans admit in foreign politics the fundamentally unchangeable quality of human affairs, and then they do it against their very nature, trying to delude

themselves that the old, discredited laws are valid only
for one emergency, one particular problem, one country,
but certainly not for all times and circumstances; otherwise all their history may become meaningless. That is
why all American experiences in international affairs can
never be considered final conquests and her future decisions can never be foreseen.

The suspense is therefore sometimes unbearable for
those who watch the course of American politics. All
is well now; peace has been saved, Europe has been
patched up, the free world is rearming, Russia has con-
ceivably been contained. But, people ask themselves, do
Americans really know and trust the reasons for their
success? Will they go on bearing the overwhelming
weight of their responsibilities? Have they changed at
all? Will the young climbers find their way to the top?

The future is to be read in the nature of America. It is,
however, more difficult to know America than any other
Western country. The Americans' picture of themselves
and of their ideals is always controversial and deceptive.
They exalt exaggerated virtues, deplore partly imaginary
sins, overpraise the nobility of the original hopes, cry
over the present betrayal, denounce the imminent ruin
of everything decent and honorable, and extol the perfect
Utopia which is only a few inventions away—all this
sometimes within the same political speech or essay.

The main obstacle to a foreigner's understanding of America is perhaps the Americans' descriptions of themselves. Travelers in the United States are at first pleasantly misled by the great wealth of oversimplified generalizations which have been fashioned in part to educate many Americans of different breed, blood, opinion, religion and origin to a common pattern. After a while, travelers think they know everything and that everything is clear and logical. Later they discover that real things, events and people can only with the greatest difficulty be fitted into the rigid pattern, that no two Americans are alike because most of them are better and worse than they describe themselves, and that, above all, they are more human and diversified than the model. Travelers are then completely baffled.

Take cooking, for instance. It is easy to learn about French, Italian, Spanish, or German cuisine: all one has to do is to enter a *bistro, trattoria, posada* or *Gasthaus* and order a meal. Restaurant food in Europe is always an improved version of what the people cook and consume at home. What is American cooking really like? Violent controversies rage on the subject. When questioned, Americans will boast of the perfection of their national dishes and the scientific perfection of their diet, will deplore the bad quality of their food, will exalt French, Italian, Chinese or Bulgarian cuisine, will defend proudly the virtue of their steaks and oysters, will lament that the secret of the old American art has been lost. Field tests are almost impossible. Only a few American restaurants serve really American food. Inexperienced foreigners usually find themselves eating imitation European food indifferently prepared. They must be invited to an American home to see and taste their first traditional dishes, and even there they are prepared only rarely, mostly on great occasions. It takes years to discover the truth that, in spite of what most Americans say, their food is potentially as good as the French and the Italian, infinitely better than the English, but that it can seldom be found, that breakfast is the safest meal at any time of the day and that American sea food is perhaps better than any other.

What is the Americans' religion, what do they really believe, what is the state of their culture, why do they behave as they do? Are Americans fundamentally for or against gambling? No authority can be trusted, no generalization can be left untested and nothing should be accepted at face value. Above all, one must not allow oneself to be misled by a natural temptation to discover America in America. Europeans (and many Americans) tend only to consider significant whatever they expect to find in America—or think is essentially American—the vastness of the horizons, the great open spaces, the wealth and size of cities, the new inventions, the new ideas and the new experiments. Many things are thought "American" which are but characteristics of a mechanical age which has flourished first and most visibly in the United States. We often forget that Europe is as "American" as America herself in this matter, and sometimes even more so—that in Europe we also discovered new drugs, drilled mountains, irrigated deserts, manufactured machinery and carried on political and social experiments. Protestants similarly forget that their religion is almost wholly contained within the Catholic Church just as Catholics forget that once, before the Reformation, there were people among them whose faith was similar in many ways to the Protestants'. All this tends to distort reality: Americans (like Protestants) and Europeans (like Catholics) sometimes behave not as they would but as the world expects them to, according to the role they think they are playing. All of us, Europeans and Americans, often forget that America is not wholly "American" but is actually much more complex, varied, ancient, unpredictable and human. Any appraisal of American future decisions based solely on the cliché of a progressive, scientific, enlightened America is bound to be grossly mistaken.

**II**

*In vain do we march with unprecedented strides to em-
pire so colossal, outvying the antique, beyond Alexander's, beyond the proudest sway of Rome. It is as if we
were somehow being endowed with a vast and more and
more thoroughly appointed body, and then left with little
or no soul.*  WALT WHITMAN

AMERICANS TIRELESSLY IMPROVE everything:
machines, buildings, medicines, techniques, means of
locomotion. Therefore I was not surprised to see, at
a first and superficial glance, that America had been wonderfully improved during my absence. Cars, skyscrapers,
prices, newspapers, policemen were much bigger. Only
the Fifth Avenue buses were smaller. Women looked
especially changed. In my time, twenty-odd years ago,
when I had first come to New York to study, it was considered improper for girls to show the natural curves
of their bodies in the swelling of their dresses, and they
used to swaddle themselves tightly lest they evoke im-
modest or lascivious visions. Now many sport long conic
breasts jutting out like tents from blouses and pullovers.
They wear these phenomenal things with ease and dignity, without impudence, ostentation, shame or lustful

intentions. They carry them under their chins with the same indifference with which soldiers carry their packs on the back. Strange and unreal breasts, they are, which neither shiver nor tremble with the motion of the body, nor change shape under their own weight, sticking out always at the same angle as the women bend or recline. I was told that some are counterfeit, but that even the true ones are compressed within a rigid frame to make them look artificial. The change was not as deep as it looked at first, I concluded. These symbolic appendages are as modest and deceptive in their special way as the defenses which disguised girls' bodies years ago, a concession to fashion and not to lust, a fiction, like the little swelling which during the Renaissance lent to the meekest men an air of conquest without, however, misleading shrewd women.

In the same way, I discovered, everything had been wonderfully improved but was fundamentally the same. Improved were the drug stores where now drugs had been reduced to an inconspicuous corner, and the whole space devoted to the contents of a Near East bazaar in picturesque confusion. Improved were the old, homely grocery stores, which are now called "super markets," with neon lights, the steaks reposing in their refrigerated showcases under spotlights like jewelry. Butchers, I was sorry to discover, no longer wore old straw hats and pencils behind the ears but dressed like surgeons ready for a major operation. Milk bottles were now cardboard containers. Automatic machines had come to dispense all sorts of hot and cold drinks, books, insurance and nylon stockings. I even saw a machine called "Changette" which changes big coins into small ones.

Wonderfully improved but recognizable was my favorite paradise, the dream world of color advertising, the shrimp-pink ladies with brassy hair, the chubby children, the vigorous men, the gracious grandmothers smacking their lips in front of cakes or shivering architectures of red gelatine, smiling ecstatically in front of pots of paint, widening their eyes in surprise in front of armchairs which turn into beds, lifting their hands to the sky in praise of magic medicines.

It was reassuring to discover that that America was still the same, pursuing happiness amidst the newest household appliances, the miraculous diets, the wonderful automobiles, the latest fashions, and still learning to be gracious and discriminating.

Naturally enough, my friends, the people I had known for years, had not improved. They were older, of course, and to tell the truth, they had never managed, even years ago, to look like characters in advertisements or in movies. The fact had disturbed me at the time. I suspected then that somewhere, perhaps very near me, in the next building, at the other party, were to be found the "real" Americans, the happy characters of fiction—tall, healthy, rich, handsome, untroubled by worries. I suspected it was my fault and that I was constitutionally

incapable of penetrating deep into the country where
I lived or that I was attracted and accepted only by
Americans who had something frail, something almost
European, in their character and tastes.

Few of the people I went to see owned the many perfect machines I had seen advertised. They shrugged their
shoulders incredulously when I asked them why. Some
of them suffered from those very diseases which I had
read had been banished by new and wonderful drugs;
some had lost their hair like the inhabitants of older and
less happy countries. Very few of the women looked
like models in *Vogue*. Nobody smacked his lips, opened
his eyes wide, lifted his hands to the sky. They had few
reasons to be surprised or delighted. Many were tired,
overworked, tormented by doubts about the war and
the atomic bomb, afraid of the future, tied to debts and
taxes. Still most of them were quietly cheerful, as they
had always been, patient, human, brave, kindly, ready
to do me a favor, curious and often sad, which is not the
way people are supposed to be in a roaring, tentacular
metropolis, in the immense and powerful cities in which
is decided the destiny of the world.

A friend of mine, who works in an advertising agency,
told me over a drink that his boss was alarmed because
the public might be getting tired of the mirages of perfection perpetually kept in front of its eyes. "You see,"
he said, "you can't keep on telling them that this year's
model is finally impeccable without implicitly confessing
that they got stuck last year. The public is recognizing
that reality is immutable, that the wonderful things they

buy are not quite as good, in many ways, as the simpler things they used to buy years ago and that nothing changes man's destiny, nothing breaks his solitude, and nothing can give him peace. My job is getting very difficult." My friend was tired and he was probably speaking only for himself. Other people told me that the public goes on buying the latest models, because the ones they own seem worthless and only the newest ones will give them peace. Still, I found that many now smile bitterly over this strange fate of theirs: this drive to go on rowing as fast as the next man, without stopping.

The taxi driver who took me from my Washington hotel to the Pentagon was very nervous and constantly looked at his watch. He was a young man in his thirties. His name was Edwin. Finally he asked permission to stop and make a telephone call. When he came back he shook his head and said: "Nothing yet. My wife is expecting a child any minute. We've got a boy already. Kids are the joy of life, don't you think? I don't care if it's a boy or girl, this time. If it weren't for her and the kid I wouldn't be working. I'd rather go fishing. They are expensive, though, kids. Do you know how much this one will cost me? Four hundred dollars. I cost my father twenty-five bucks. What do you think, were they happier years ago when kids cost only twenty-five bucks? Look at my father: he had a 1929 Chevrolet, second-hand, and kept it till he died. He cleaned it, polished it, fixed it himself, kept it in excellent condition. I have to trade in my car almost every year. I get to be ashamed of the old car and feel happy only when I've got the new model. What do you think?"

Many Americans talk about fishing with the suspicious insistence with which middle-aged Frenchmen with stomach trouble talk about food and middle-aged Italians about love. *New York Times* editorials, Ernest Hemingway's books, many magazine articles, a good part of current humor and conversation are dedicated to fish. Businessmen stop in front of shop windows filled with tackle like the hungry in front of restaurants or the lonely in front of penny-arcade machines. Stuffed fish on the wall are religious objects or patron saints protecting rooms in which men gather to use bawdy language and drink. Many who spoke to me about their sport and who described with glittering eyes their past and future trips seldom looked as if they could be comfortable in the open air under a tent. Some were soft-bellied, with false teeth, pale as *champignons*, and were probably kept alive by pills and careful management. They undoubtedly took on their trips the bright new store clothes of Miss Rheingold, the complicated gear of the wealthy dilettante, and had to be nursed by attentive and respectful guides. Why was fishing so important?

Others talk with the same nostalgia of gardening, farming and living in the country. A taxi driver in New York wanted to raise chickens, and we talked, while waiting for a green light on 57th Street, about Leghorns, black and white. If it hadn't been for his wife and her expensive habits, he told me, he would have given up driving. Many people I knew had left the cities for the real country, hours away. An important New York doctor had gone to live in an obscure Pennsylvania village, where he bought a farm and now tries hard to fit in local life, defending local traditions and institutions, curious about local history, and taking a snobbish pride in trying to pass for a native. He gently despises those who arrived after him.

The wife of an R.K.O. official left Hollywood last year and bought herself a flour mill in the Ozark Mountains. The mill is more than one hundred years old, of the story-book kind moved by a stream of water which turns the big wooden wheel and surrounded by very old trees. This lady started milling flour as a joke, grinding the wheat between the two millstones and selling it to friends who liked the old taste of bread and cakes. Now she is doing good business by mail. Her husband showed me some glossy pictures of well-known R.K.O. movie stars playing about his wife's mill. He had ordered the photos to help advertise the flour, and he told me that next year he too would retire to the Ozarks and dedicate himself to manufacturing and selling stone-ground products in picturesque post-card surroundings.

All this, the fish, the farming, the simple village life, the rough clothes, the local traditions, the ancient ballads, were genuine and honest but always left me ill at ease. Nobody I know in Rome, in Venice, in Florence or in Naples wants really to get away or go fishing that badly. Some do, but they go without talking about it, as a matter of course. They prefer another life, and they never surround themselves with the paraphernalia and the souvenirs of their chosen trade or hobby as if they were relics, and they certainly would not order publicity pictures filled with movie stars of their secret hideaways. There is, of course, in all this, something more: the Petit Trianon with milkmaids and shepherds, Arcadia, the nostalgia of paralytics for long walks, of prisoners for angels' wings, of the damned for the earthly paradise they left behind. Truly, the American countryside is the most beautiful I have ever seen, the only one in which one forgets the existence of man that is always at your elbow in Europe. Lonely rivers wander majestically between woods as old as the world, woods such as only children can imagine. Life in the American villages, in the small cities and in the provinces is warm, cordial and gay. People gossip, visit each other, still meet by chance in the streets, welcome strangers with courtesy, are ready to help, mourn, or rejoice with their friends. The food is often good, the tempo of life is often slow, and there is time for conversation and thinking. Loneliness, cruelty, indifference, boredom, the sense of one's tragic impotence and uselessness seem to dominate life only in the big cities.

Foreigners are convinced that the hard life of the cities is the American life and that Americans really prefer canned food, slogans, comics, neon lights and the anonymity of immense organizations. All comparisons between life in the United States and in Europe stop at the big cities, mostly at New York. No foreign traveler seems to suspect that many Americans are uncomfortable in their own world. I first discovered this when I visited Mr. Henry Ford many years ago. He had invited me to lunch at the suggestion of his press office—as I was then correspondent of the *Corriere della Sera*—at the factory's restaurant in the big executives' dining room. Ford was one of the world's great heroes, who had given his country the large factory, the conveyor belt, mass production. Europeans then envied Ford, who had transformed his country and the rest of the world. He looked old and absent-minded, spoke little and ate hurriedly. He had the white silky hair of an eighteenth-century French abbé and looked frail and small. His clothes hung emptily as if his arms and legs were of steel wire like those of mechanical puppets. Somebody told me he had abandoned all active work and only dabbled sometimes in his private laboratory where he was trying to run a steam engine from the heat developed by the radiator of a gasoline motor.

He came to life first when I asked him whether his system of production did not humiliate men. He said proudly that his workers were happy, that if they wanted to write symphonies and poems they would not be in his factory, that in medieval Europe they would be the poor, starving hired hands, and that there was far more standardization in European peasants than among his men. His eyes sparkled when he showed me his museum. It was stored in a large factory building and was a strange collection of things no more than fifty, sixty, or eighty years old, the hand-worked water pumps, the ancient pedal sewing machines, decorated with colored flowers and cupids, the red fire engines, the potbellied stoves, the buggies, and one beautiful train of yellow coaches hand-painted with romantic landscapes of waterfalls, woods, and beaches.

Coming, as I did, from an industrially backward and thrifty country, most of those things I had been living with all my life. Some had filled the seaside villas of my childhood vacations, and some I had left behind a few weeks before. Italy did not possess hand-painted trains, of course, but Sicily was filled with hand-painted horse carts. The idea of placing all those ordinary objects in a museum puzzled me. What was the meaning of such a collection? There was a little orchestra at one side, in the museum, playing American old-fashioned dance tunes, and many boys, workers' sons, were learning square dances. That was what Mr. Ford had come to watch. We stopped a while. Finally he said, "You're from Italy, aren't you? We'll ask them to play my favorite Italian song." I thought it was going to be "O Sole Mio," or "Funiculi Funicula," one of those tunes all Americans know, or an opera aria, perhaps by Verdi. It wasn't. It was a forgotten song—"Ciribiribin"—which my grandmother had hummed, romantic, *espiègle*, roguish, which suited the charcoal-warmed irons and copper bed warmers of the museum. Mr. Ford conducted the music, lifting his empty sleeves and pale hands while humming the tune.

Then I understood that the museum was dedicated to the world he loved and had destroyed with his own hands. He actually disliked the world as "Fordismus" had left it, and he was trying to atone as best he could. That was his tomb, where he, like the ancient Pharaohs, had gathered all the things that he had cherished in life, and they were not the products of modern factories. Mr. Ford, like many Americans, did not feel comfortable in the paradise he had worked earnestly all his life to build.

The ladies used to shut their eyes at bullfights years ago and always said they were disgusting, brutal, barbarian exhibitions. The men always said they were on the side of the bull and wanted to see the *torero* killed. Why have bullfights acquired such disturbing importance in American life? Books, movies, paintings, essays are continually dedicated to the game. At most summer fights in Spain an unusual number of seats is always reserved for American travelers. At the San Isidro fights last May, my section was so completely American (the tickets around me had been reserved for hotel *con-*

*cierges*) that I could have been in Yankee Stadium. Bullfights are a flamboyant denial of American polite ideals.
They are cruel to animals, they are inefficient and wasteful ways of butchering cattle, and they are a proud
affirmation that man's only important qualities are his
courage, his mastery over his fear and over nature's
furies. They are an elegant game played with human
lives, the apotheosis of death.

Death is not important in the American scene. Death
is rouged, combed, and dressed by the undertakers, death
is surrounded by the solemn and sanitary paraphernalia
of medical science, death is barely mentioned in prayers
and sermons. Death in the movies and in the theater is
seldom shown and recognizable. Do Americans realize the
importance of things they have kept hidden from themselves, like sweepings pushed under sofas, but never quite
forgotten? Do Americans suspect that their destiny is
that of every man and their only weapons the old
virtues?

Years ago important Americans of another generation
worked hard, despised loafers, never wasted a minute,
were punctual in their offices, for their appointments,
whether at the club for the Turkish bath and the rub-
down, at dinner in their boiled shirts, or at the theater;
they were relentless and sleepless. The amount of work
they did was Homeric: they were building the imperial,

industrial and powerful nation we know, and they had no time to lose. They were also establishing their private fortunes. On Saturdays and Sundays they wore knee-length breeches and woolen stockings like boys and ran over meadows, behind a golf ball, to which, from time to time, they gave blows strong enough to kill an ox. Every day most of them drank half a quart of whisky, some more and some less, which represented for them what, for other people, were concubines, philosophy, hashish, adventure, consolations, love and poetry.

Then, one day, between their fiftieth and sixtieth year, at their desks, on the golf course, negotiating a difficult deal, or in the Turkish bath, they suddenly stopped talking, turned purple, gasped for air, and died of heart failure.

Many of their wives are still alive. These old ladies who were, on an average, five or ten years younger than their husbands, will live to very old age, having taken good care of themselves all their lives: long hours of sleep in the morning, a nap just before dinner for their complexions, regular trips to Europe, lazy cruises to warm seas in the winter, scientific diets, unimportant love affairs with Continental Europeans whose names they soon forgot. (Many of them keep an Italian sky-blue cavalry cape somewhere and some of them still wear it in the evening.) They are now well preserved and as recognizable as flowers kept within the pages of a book. Many have no home: the sons and daughters are married and separated from them by an abyss of misunderstanding, the husband buried, incomes reduced by taxes, the problem of finding servants and keeping them—all this has made them rent, abandon or sell everything. They tour hotels and *pensions* in the United States, the West Indies and Europe. Many are to be found in the little hotels in the East Fifties, in New York, where they are well taken care of like pets in a pet shop. One day, when I was living in one of those hotels, the fire alarm rang for a test atomic attack and we all had to troop to the rallying point. I never thought there could be so many of them. Some came on their wheel chairs, some in mink coats, some with diamonds around their neck, some clutching little jewelry cases, all very old, fretting, worried, nervous. They are very wealthy and powerful, I was told, as they own the majority of shares in many great corporations. They alone can afford expensive things and have a taste for them left—jewelry, antiques, precious furs, Paris gowns—all the things that one can see in the shops of the quarter they inhabit.

All this was new to me. The East Fifties were at my time the kingdom of gilded youth; debutantes and boys down from the good colleges, the pretty actresses and dancing girls in the speakeasies, the night clubs, and the expensive little shops with the intimate names like Lily, Albertino, Ischia, Jean, or Elaine. Now you mostly see grandmothers curled like champion dogs ready for the show, tied in iron straps like cotton bales, dressed with vaporous Paris dresses created a few weeks before for young brides. And then one notices that everything around has aged with the ladies. The smart hotels of twenty years ago are decomposing slowly: wash basins are cracked, taps drip, the furniture sags, the elevators whine painfully. The waiters are still the same, as no new ones have come from Europe in years. Some are decrepit, and drag their flat feet with a wan smile, or so deaf that one has to shout orders in their ears. One of them said to me, "*Eh, in Italia le cose si fanno meglio,* things are done better in Italy." He had left Rome in 1907 and had never gone back. His Rome no more exists than the New York he had seen when he had landed in his youth, but it was still alive in his thoughts, a mere term for comparisons.

Walking about one sometimes thought of Venice and her quaint little shops filled with delicate and useless laces and glassware, of Belgrave Square, of the rue de Rivoli, with its little hotels where Charles Dickens or Giovacchino Rossini stopped, of other quarters and cities which had aged with the world which had given them life. The chic East Fifties will soon be as historical as the Vieux Carré in New Orleans, relics, like the widows and the waiters, of other elegances, ideals, morals, hopes and prides.

Newport was very handsome in the early autumn sun. The great parks looked ancient. The trees were inordinately high, their foliage was rich and glossy and the lawns were well groomed. Nobody seemed to be around. There were no voices. In the silence there was the hum of a distant mower and the muted roar of the sea. The great and famous houses which, fifty years ago, had been ridiculed by European snobs, did not now look incongruous in their painstaking imitations of foreign styles. With age they had acquired dignity. As if deposited there by a miraculous wind, Scotch medieval castles stood side by side with rococo pavilions from Versailles, Medici villas from the hills of Florence, English manors with oak beams on the façade and châteaux from Touraine. They were mostly closed and looked empty. No children played in the gardens, no horses looked out of the stables, no maid was to be seen at the upstairs windows, no butler polished silver at the downstairs windows.

I paid a dollar to see the most famous, Cornelius Vanderbilt's "Breakers," which is now in the care of the Newport Historical Society. The owner, the Countess Szechenyi née Vanderbilt, who lives in a little flat in the village, could not afford to keep it up. The municipal tax alone amounted to $15,000, which is probably less than many parties cost in the old days. I wandered through the seventy bedrooms (of which thirty-three were for servants), observed the chandeliers piped for gas and wired for electricity, the salt- and fresh-water plumbing, watched the sea from Mr. Vanderbilt's bedroom, and lingered reverently in the salons, which are the most sumptuous, rich, complicated and elaborate I have ever seen. Only the imagination of a society-mad author of nineteenth-century boudoir novels could have invented such improbable splendor, which is somewhere between an Austrian watering hole, a palace of an Oriental monarch only recently introduced to Western wonders, and a residence of a demi-mondaine under the Third Republic. Vanderbilt imported three hundred Italians for the marble and stucco work, and most of them stayed on, founding an important local colony. They introduced to Newport the old game of *bocce*, which is still played in the back yard of the Reading Room, the venerable local club, by members shouting the correct Italian words. They do so probably for the same reasons that Italian noblemen who play golf in Rome cry "Fore" to the ruins of the imperial aqueducts.

People still live in many of the great Newport houses, I was told, but primarily weak and old people who rarely go out and cannot be seen from the outside. Many of them carry on the old existence as if nothing had happened: the four- or five-course dinners on the ancient vermeil dishes, the hothouse grapes and the orchids, the two or three good wines, and the dull conversation under the priceless Gobelin and the Italian primitive for which Berenson has a kind word somewhere. Around them still silently move a few old servants who remember the gestures and the courtesies of fifty years ago. When these people die (some always die at the first cold of autumn, I was told; three had died the week before my visit) the house is shuttered, the hothouse stoves are put out for the first time, the orchids freeze and the old servants are dismissed with their legacies. The younger generation, the sons, grandsons, and great-grandsons of the owners, generally refuse to manage villas as complicated and expensive as hotels or to pay the necessary taxes out of their diminished incomes. Even those who could afford it no longer enjoy living a life so laborious and magnificent, for which they have no taste and have not been trained. The villas are then put up for sale. A few have been sold to Catholic convents and schools. Others have been left to institutions. Many more await a buyer.

The owners worry a lot about the future of their houses. They dream of leaving everything as it is—the paintings, the ancient woodwork imported from some French château, the English silver, the enameled snuff-boxes, the carpets and the statues—to some museum or college which would promise to preserve them for future generations. They talk endlessly about this, studying prospective heirs, exploring possibilities. But institutions do not accept such gifts unless they are accompanied by an endowment sufficient to keep them up, and many old owners are now saving money, cutting out unnecessary expenses, firing old retainers, in order to put aside a little fund, the dowry which is to save their dear house from irreverence and destruction.

My first dinner in Newport impressed me greatly. The house was simpler than those I had visited during the day. It belonged to an old family that had gathered there all their old things, the furniture and the portraits, some very good and some bad, but obviously not selected at the same time. The hosts were pleasant and polite. They knew people in Rome and had relatives in Italy. Newport had been the principal place where, before the First

World War, European noblemen had flocked in great numbers, hunting for rich American wives. This has left behind some old friendships and complicated relationships, cousins two or three times removed who visit each other sometimes and rarely know what to speak about. For the same reason, in old villas in Italy, one occasionally runs across libraries filled with American novels of the nineties and bound volumes of old American magazines, American paintings, and sometimes fine American antiques which belonged to some dead great-grandmother.

A white-haired major-domo directed four liveried footmen with imperious gestures. A white-coated barman mixed drinks in the drawing room before and after dinner. The wines were good and the food was formal. I was impressed. Such magnificence, I thought, must have cost in America what, in Europe, would have paid for the entertaining of a private army. How could these people afford such luxury at the present time? In the following days, however, everything was clear. In every house where I was invited, the white-haired major-domo, the four footmen, the white-coated barman, whom everybody called "Fido," the good wines, the formal food were always the same. The servants were a little touring company enacting "the good old days" each time in a different set.

The beautiful ladies with naked shoulders, the gallant men murmuring reassuring compliments, the grave husbands talking about business, the witty bachelors who shocked everybody with their stories were all over fifty years of age. I never saw the younger generations. (There were framed photographs of earnest, younger people here and there on the tables, some of them in uniform.) I was told the young rarely came. They were in New York, in Boston, in Philadelphia, working; they were in college; they had government jobs in Washington; they were in the Army—in Germany or in Korea; they were running experimental farms; they were breeding fur-bearing animals. The conversation around me was idle and gracious. *Bons mots* were said in polite French. People talked disrespectfully of Harry Truman, damned the memory of Franklin Roosevelt, spoke harshly about the Marshall Plan which, they said, had encouraged Europe to think that America was a bottomless pit, or made fun of some noble new project they had read about in the papers. Over American military expenses they were sharply divided, some wanting them cut to the bone and some wanting them kept at about the same level in order to defeat the communists. Everybody agreed that the money was being spent recklessly and that the same results could have been reached with more care.

An important financier, a man of action, who looked vaguely like George Washington, took me by the arm one evening and led me to the bar for a drink. He said: "Let 'em talk. They know nothing. They don't live in the contemporary world. They don't know what has happened to them. We've had a revolution in America. These people have had their heads cut off like the French aristocrats, only not with the guillotine but with the income tax. You know, nobody likes the rich any more in this country. They used to love them when I was a boy. Our own children don't want to be reminded that they are rich. They hate all these things, the Aubusson carpets, the *bois-de-rose* marquetry, the Irish hunters and the gardens that need the work of at least ten men. They are right. What's important today is working, ordinary, everyday, honest people." He turned and smiled to the barman, "Isn't it a fact, Fido, that we have been good friends for thirty-five years?" Then he said to me, "This is real American democracy. Fido and I have been good friends for thirty-five years." Fido said Yes, that they had been real friends for thirty-five years, and went to fetch clean glasses.

I asked, "What's Fido's real name?"

The financier shrugged his shoulders and said, "Fido? I don't know. I've always called him Fido."

Mrs. F., a middle-aged, well-read lady, who is passionately preoccupied about her country, told me the following story. Her daughter, who is taking a course in dramatics in college, had been given the last act of Thornton Wilder's *Our Town* to study. She came home with the book and, after dinner, started reading out loud to her father and mother. After a while she could not go on. Her eyes filled with tears. Then Mrs. F. took the book from her hands and continued. After reading a few pages she also stopped. She was crying. Mr. F., who is a man of letters, not easily moved by words alone, made fun of his women and took the book. He read on but soon his voice choked and his glasses became misty. Mrs. F. told me, "You see, I realized that that was my country as it used to be, the country I had grown up in, as I remembered it from my youth."

"I," said the lady with the new teeth, looking at me straight in the eyes, "adore nature. And you?" She leaned toward me as if to catch my answer and showed the flabby and wrinkled skin of her chest pinched by invisible bands. A little old man, dressed in a new and well-pressed pistachio-colored suit, said, "I love the sea." The others nodded.

All around us, in the shabby and coquettish living room, groups of middle-aged people, well off, provincial, dressed obviously in their best clothes, were making embarrassingly sincere conversation. Behind a potted plant an old lady was saying, "I am a gypsy at heart." A fat woman with glasses said, "My religion is the Sermon on the Mount. That's all anyone should need." Finally Miss Claire Elaine (this is not her true name but similar to that which she used in her advertisements) came from the kitchen carrying a tray and cried, "Eats, eats . . . Everybody stop flirting . . . We've got hot biscuits, cinnamon toast, tea, and ice cream for those who like it. Yum, yum!" All the women surrounded the tray, as

women usually do, busying themselves filling cups, pouring hot water, cutting the cake, and handing out dishes.
The men sat silently, empty-eyed, waiting. One nervous
old man leaned toward me and asked, "How are things
really in Europe?"

It was a Sunday afternoon in Los Angeles. The downtown streets were empty and silent. Our voices rang in
the house as in a sound stage. I did not know anyone
there and probably would never see any of them again
the rest of my life. Nevertheless, I did not have the courage to get up, tell them what I thought of them and
leave. I played the game, confessed that I also believed
in God, that friendship between a man and a woman
was sometimes possible, hoped there wouldn't be a third
World War, and ate curious biscuits with a white coco-
nut wig on them.

I was there under false pretenses, a traitor, and I was
ashamed of myself now that I was looking at their earnest and honest faces. I had found the address that morning in the Los Angeles *Mirror*. It said, "Are you lonely?
Claire Elaine, national organization, exclusive social club,
high class, parties every Sunday afternoon." There were
many other similar advertisements but Claire Elaine attracted me. I had telephoned, I had explained that I was
a traveling foreigner far from home, and I had taken a
taxi at the appointed time. The abandoned little street
with the row of Spanish-style cottages, fashionable thirty
years ago, the living room with its worn-out furniture,
the chintz, the satin pillows, and the good people with
glasses making conversation, troubled me. They were

anxious to have a quiet good time. In their eyes you could read the fear of not making the right impression, of leaving as alone as they had come, friendless, with nobody to talk to.

California is for the United States what the United States is for the rest of us, a clean new world, where everything is easy and possible, where the embarrassing traditions and the errors of the past are forgotten, the empty slate on which to start writing anew. Industries are developing there faster than anywhere else at any time. The wilderness is blossoming. Gigantic dams and irrigation projects have opened deserts to cultivation. Poor men have become rich in a few years. There are more jobs than people, and the newspapers are filled with large advertisements asking for draftsmen, electricians and all kinds of specialists. In five years the fifth largest state of the union has become the second. Population and per capita wealth increase hand in hand. The cities of the East and Middle West look, in perspective, like the old English and German towns must have appeared to the men who had left them for America in past centuries: dusty, old, resigned, cynical, tired, set. To be in California now is a thrilling experience, like being in Virginia or Massachusetts before the Revolution or in Chicago in the seventies or eighties. There is the same confidence in the future, the same confusion, the same raw pleasures and the same moving hopes of better days.

People flock to Southern California with every bus, plane and train. There the climate is mild, life easy, opportunities unlimited. You don't have to dress in Los Angeles. Dressing is a worn-out prejudice, a feudal practice. All you need is a pair of pants, a colored sports shirt with some lively scene depicted in vigorous colors, a pair of sandals, sunglasses and a car to travel back and forth on the smooth highways, from the sea to the snowy mountains, from the orange groves to the desert. You don't have to leave the car at all, unless you want to sleep in a bed. People eat in drive-in restaurants, go to drive-in movies. Everybody is sunburned, everybody looks happy.

Among the technicians, the speculators, the dreamers, the earnest, ambitious and adventurous young people who arrive, there is also a great number of idle old people who come not to build a new world but to live the last years of their lives in comfort. Most of them are well off: widows who have inherited money, farmers who have sold their farms, parents who have been pensioned off by their sons and divorcees who spend their alimonies. They live in little rented houses, in *pensions*, in hotels, in furnished rooms. They are everywhere. The restaurants are filled with them. They line up in front of movie palaces waiting for the first feature. They crowd the shops, play golf, sit on park benches, tour about in their cars—restless and sad old people who have nothing to do all day. If life is to be conceived as a greasy pole, this, for them, is the top, where the bottles, the chickens and the hams are strung. If life is a race, Los Angeles is for them the finish line where the prizes are awarded. This is where the rainbow ends, this is where the pot of gold is buried, this is where the Holy Grail is kept, this is the end of the trail, this is the last frontier where the trek west stops in front of the ocean.

You look at the old men in their canvas baseball caps and sunglasses, the old women with the fancy trousers and the greenish false teeth, the poor people who don't know what to do with themselves, who have everything money can buy and industry, science and advertising can provide—new machines, new diets, new medicines, new religions, wonderful movies, the best climate in the world—and wonder whether they would be more or less miserable dead, or in Europe or in other centuries. Their ancestors crossed the Atlantic on sailing ships, cleared the forests, trekked west in covered wagons, fought the Indians, and everywhere they had to create civilization once again: build the houses, the churches, the schools, the saloons, import the first piano, the first books, the first machinery. They had to go on without waiting for their new cities to be finished, on to something else, tirelessly, until they reached another ocean. And here they were.

Here they were, in Miss Claire Elaine's drawing room, eating cake and ice cream, hoping to find a wife or a husband, somebody to talk to in the darkness of the night, in their big beds, hoping that life was not all movies, candies, television, diets, gadgets, medicines, science, but something else. I thought how pleasant cold weather can be, sometimes, and how one does not feel snow falling on one's shoulders when talking to a sweetheart or

working hard, and how good is unscientific bread out of
an unscientific oven, even in the United States. I thought
how busy many grandmothers are who know the recipes
and the stories. One elderly woman with shining glasses
asked me how old I was, what my name was, whether I
was married, how many children I had. She was eager
and shameless in her interest and grabbed my sleeve
when she feared somebody else would try to get me
away from her. I was embarrassed and afraid. When we
left she apologized, "You know, you remind me of a
boy of mine who died in Italy during the war." It was
probably true.

Another advertisement in the newspaper merely said,
"Psychoanalysis." Then there were the words (carefully
selected to avoid penalties for false representation),
"State licensed, expert, confidential." Nothing was
promised. No degrees were mentioned. I made an appointment by telephone and went. The address was that
of a small office building in downtown Los Angeles.
Along the corridors there were glass doors with the
names of theatrical agents, massage experts, one yogi,
one teacher of jujitsu and one teacher of guitar. The "expert and confidential" psychologist was a very young
man, probably just out of the Army. He sat in a little
cubbyhole, behind his desk. The wall was covered with
green paper dotted with tiny flowers. A majolica object,
two milk-colored fawns' heads, in the taste of Christmas
cards or fairy-tale illustrations, hung on one side. On the
other there was a little bookstand containing ordinary

schoolbooks. A corner was occupied by a new couch, scientifically designed to follow the curves of the body, which was being advertised in all papers that week.

The young man looked at me with confidential eyes and said, "Yes?" I told him about my case. I had made up a few symptoms on the way. He tapped the desk with his pencil as I talked and nodded, as if nothing I could say would surprise him. His shirt was clean but wrinkled; he probably washed it in the evening, before going to bed, and had nobody to iron it for him. Finally he said, "Reality is not what we imagine. What we see is not usually what there is at all. Our wishes, our fears, our illusions, and our emotions distort our perceptions. We try to fight something which may not be there. Perhaps you are adapting your behavior to a nonexistent reality. You are struggling against obstacles which exist only in your mind, and don't perceive what really is troubling your life." He took a book from the stand without moving and showed it to me. It was an ordinary high-school science textbook. It fell open at a page on which there were old drawings showing optical illusions, the stairs that go either up or down, the parallel lines which seem to converge. He showed them to me as if they were something new. He said, "You see here two faces looking at each other, don't you? Well, if you look at them steadily you will also see a bird bath. There. I told you." Apparently that was all the science behind his reassuring façade. He told me a few case histories proving that his intervention had made people happy, had given timid men a will to conquer life, had given lonely ladies a rea-

son to go on living. He had snatched tired people from
suicides' graves. Everybody he had cured by showing
them that life was a great optical illusion, and, for all I
knew, he might have been right. I paid ten dollars. Just
before our interview was over the door opened and a
middle-aged woman appeared, with dyed red hair, a Ha-
waiian shirt and flannel trousers. Her eyes were red as
though she had been crying. The young expert rudely
chased her away. "Don't bother me now, Mrs. Griffith,"
he barked at her with a new voice. "Wait a minute.
Don't you see I'm busy?" The lady apologized humbly
and closed the door. When I went out she hurriedly ran
in.

If the life surrounding us is always yesterday's cold
revolution, if what we consider obvious or "self-evi-
dent" today, was whispered mysteriously thirty or forty
years ago by long-haired intellectuals, debated in col-
lege-town cafés or shouted over barricades, the future
should be easy to read in what the young do, think and
hate. What are, for example, these frail and cumbersome
international organizations whose main purpose seems
to be to reassure us with kind words, if not the university dreams of the generation of Franklin Roosevelt,
Edouard Beneš, Gaetano Salvemini, Clement Attlee?

Many young Americans of my student days were
either cynical or revolutionary. The cynics wanted to

plunge into the struggle, conquer success at any price and set aside a good number of dollars. The revolutionary wanted to blow everything up with dynamite, drown everything in a blood bath, because everything was corrupt and false. The two hopes sprang perhaps from the same resignation in front of the disease of the time, an incurable disease which had either to be wiped out with violence, or exploited by the ambitious who wanted to fatten on it like trees planted on a graveyard. My contemporaries wrote beautiful books. Some were astutely designed like word machines to attract the greatest number of readers, others were livid and brutal accusations of the contemporary world. Where are the young Americans of today, what do they believe, what are their hopes?

The old lady with the blue-tinted gray hair asked me by all means never to speak to her about her daughter. "She is very queer," she said and started talking very fast about the war that would undoubtedly break out next year, provoked by the shape of sunspots. I never know what people mean when they say "queer." It may be any deviation from the norm, but the range is very wide, from picking one's nose to a penchant for necrophilia. I asked, "Queer? What happened to her?" The daughter I remembered was a polite, quiet, pale girl. The old lady explained that she now lived very modestly in a little flat on what she made with her work, that she had a job writing advertisements for a department store, that she was very earnest and was engaged to a young man who was writing dramas for television. As the family was well-to-do, all these virtuous efforts seemed out of place to the old lady.

"We laugh at those who ruin themselves trying to pretend they have more money than they really have. I think it's just as bad taste to make believe you're poor when you really aren't," said the old lady. "My daughter is an inverted snob. Sometimes I try to give her old things of mine, jewels, a carpet, silver. She sends everything back saying that she doesn't want her life cluttered up with possessions."

This was told to me by a friend who happened to be there. On state road 41, just out of Atlanta, Georgia, in an abandoned roadhouse, a group of students meets regularly. One night a while ago, they arrived a few at a time, leaving their old cars parked outside, and sat in silence on four rows of chairs in front of a naked table. The last to come sat on the floor. Beer and soft-drink advertisements were still hanging from the wall; in the empty lunchroom, pretty girls grinning over bottles. Robert L. West, an eighteen-year-old boy, with a purple velvet coat, a bow tie and flannel trousers, came in, turned off the lights, and stood behind the table, like a chemistry teacher ready to start an experiment. On the table were two lighted candles and a large white crucifix. West opened the Bible and said, "I ask you to look at this symbol, the cross, because it is the most important

symbol of our world. It is the symbol of sorrow and sacrifice. Sorrow and sacrifice will be the fate of some of
us, perhaps of most of us. But sorrow and sacrifice are
of no use and have no meaning if we have not the courage to ask the help of God, to dedicate sorrow and sacrifice to God. We young people are ready to do anything we can do with our hands and with our head.
That's not enough. Maybe we're too cowardly to work
with God." Robert West was a student, like the others,
who felt within him the vocation to preach. His sermons
were followed by many of his companions, some of
whom gave up movies, dancing or moonlight rides to
listen to him. He talked quietly, without the terrifying
words of the popular preacher.

The plane for Los Angeles was two hours late from
Chicago. A storm was raging. Squalls of wind and rain
shook the doors of the airport waiting room. There were
few people there, at three o'clock in the morning: the
air-line employees in uniform yawning behind their
desks, a hostess who had just got up and was wide
awake, clean and brisk, a sleeping Negro on a bench
curled up in his coat, a mother with her child in her
arms, a young Army officer and myself. The officer was
from Boston. He said to me, "Our fathers and grandfathers thought they had a marshal's baton in their knap-
sack or were born with a contract in their pockets which

said: wealth and happiness are guaranteed to you. You, in Europe, cannot have an idea of this old American feeling, that everything came to the man who worked hard, that he was to marry the prettiest girl in town and live a lifelong honeymoon, that he was never to grow old, that he was always to have the most modern and expensive house filled with gadgets, and a full bank account. Since all these could not be had, life being what it is, people always felt a little cheated because the things they managed to get were never as good as the things they had wanted, and everybody felt that somehow Providence had not kept faith with them. It's different with us, the men of my generation. We live without knowing if we'll be alive at Christmas, if we'll see next year, if we'll ever become old. Take me. I had just finished college. Then I was called up. I had a few months to say good-bye to my old life and my ambitions. I didn't dramatize; I didn't get drunk. I carried on as if nothing had happened. I'm going to Tokyo, then probably to Korea. Am I scared? Maybe. Years ago, the younger generation were pacifists and wanted to abolish war. We hate war as much as they did but we know there is nothing we can do. Whoever has to go, goes."

Dorothy was, fifteen years ago, the belle of the ball, capricious, fickle, adorable and boring as a child. She is now a handsome and quiet married lady who drives a rusty old car. She lives in the suburbs in a rented house which is old-fashioned and needs a new coat of paint. She is married to a lawyer, a dry and polite man. They have five children. They have no servants. Every morning Dorothy gets breakfast for seven, makes seven beds, sends the bigger children to school, takes care of the younger ones, dusts, washes, irons, cooks, sews buttons, darns, sweeps, and this for six days a week. On Wednesday, her day off, a neighborhood girl takes care of the children and Dorothy drives to New York, where she goes shopping, visits friends or takes in a show. On Saturday and Sunday her husband stays home and works hard mending everything that needs mending—clogged sinks, dripping faucets—paints the furniture, doors and walls, or fixes all the gadgets and the machinery that went wrong during the week. One night Dorothy invited me to dinner. The dinner was very good. Everything had been cooked by her, including the bread, because, she said, "You can't eat store bread any more." The children were well behaved and silent and disappeared before dinner. She is happy. What does she hope? She hopes her husband will soon become a partner in his firm. Then what? They will then have a little more money and may have a sixth child. Nothing else? Does she regret the old easy life, the parties, the trips to Europe, the servants? No. She regrets nothing.

Rupert Allan, of the Los Angeles bureau of *Look*, told me the following story: "A friend of mine came out of

the war troubled by a profound moral crisis. He wanted
to think. He found a little house in the country, far from
everything, to figure things out. He took along no
books, only notebooks and pencils. He took long walks
during the day, all alone, and, at night, sat down and
wrote. After several months he had filled several notebooks with valuable thoughts. He believed he had understood important things. With his notebooks filled with
words he went to see an old teacher of his, asking him
to read what he had written. The teacher read and said,
'My compliments, my boy. I'm surprised. You have gone
from Hume to Locke all by yourself. You haven't
reached Kant yet but you may get there with a little
more effort.' "

The pretty young Hollywood actress took her shoes
off and sighed. We were sitting in a producer's garden in
Beverly Hills one night. A small party was going on in
the house. The girl was slightly drunk and very, very
sad. Things were going badly, she said. She couldn't get
a certain part in a picture, she was tired, she wanted to
rest, she had no money to go on a trip. "Is living worth-
while?" she asked me. "I know the limits of my success.
I'm no fool. I don't dream wealth and glory. Many
small parts, from now on, some good, some bad, parts
which they could have given to any one of twenty other
girls, then old age. I've seen the old girls. They have a

gin bottle in the bathroom. To get those damned bit parts you have to work hard. You must be pretty, charming and well groomed. They must see you everywhere. You must always smile. The taxes take away what you could save and which would give you time to study and choose. Do we know what will happen to us tomorrow? Should I get married, have children, build a house in which to grow old? What do you think? No. I know it. That's why we drink. I'll grow old sooner, maybe. I'll die sooner. Let the damned A-bomb come and let's get it over with."

The professor teaches Greek and philosophy at the University of Chicago. He's a handsome, gray-haired man, patient and wise, dressed in the intellectual's tweeds of thirty years ago. We sat in his study at the end of his day. It was an ancient English-Gothic room, with windows of opaque glass panes held together with lead strips, and carved walnut furniture, like Oxford. I asked him about the youth of today. The professor knocked the ashes from his pipe and said, "They are strange young people. There are no iconoclasts among them, for one thing; nobody who declares that Plato is a fool and philosophy a useless waste of time. The young people, in my time, knew that the world began with them and that everything had to be invented all over again. They made a bonfire of everything, traditions, rules, laws. They wrote prose without punctuation and capitals, poetry without sense. They drank a lot and struggled mightily against the temptations of virtue. The young people of today have nothing to destroy. They have no heroes to imitate or to demolish, which is about the same thing. They are mostly timid conformists or conservatives who don't know what to conform to or what to preserve. They study with great diligence, try to understand, try to follow some rules, like those who, in the spring, play the first game of tennis on a court whose lines have been washed away by winter storms. Our young new writers are good technicians, which again is a sign of timidity. They write doubtful and cautious things, as if they were afraid to be deceived by life. Many of them believe that deception is the only certainty, that *le pire est toujours certain*, which is a strange faith for Americans to have. In conclusion, I feel they want to believe firmly in something but don't really know what."

Generations do not brutally succeed one another, like the acts of a drama, but together occupy the stage for a long time, each reading its own private lines, the younger taking on more and more room and authority as the older gradually shrinks and fades away. Three generations can be discerned in the United States today, as well defined and as clearly different as geological strata.

The architecture of the Older Generation is the neo-classical style of Thomas Jefferson and the Founding Fathers: Ionic columns carved out of solid marble, heavy mahogany doors, real leather armchairs, bronze grillework and brass spittoons, the style of the more solid banks, the big railway stations, the better clubs, and the United States Senate Office Building. Respectful Negroes wait on the Old Generation at table, in the businessmen's clubs, in the private compartments of transcontinental trains, in the Senate restaurant. As they get off their Pullman cars, the Old Generation always extend their feet to the Negro porters who wipe their shoes one after another; the gesture is probably an ancient one, going back to the days when traveling Americans' feet were dusty, and it reminds one of the India of the *pukkah sahibs*, Czarist Russia, or feudal Hungary. The Old Generation believe in laissez faire, in free competition in almost all business activities, mostly other people's, but in good tariff barriers for their own; they are against excessive expenditures, unbalanced budgets and too ambitious a foreign policy. The new imperial responsibilities have troubled and divided them. Some knew that the day would come in which America had to run the world. It had been foreseen by wise Americans for the last hundred years and did not come as a surprise. Others curse the fate which has tossed such weights onto the shoulders of the American people. They all grumble about heavy taxes—even the poor, who pay little or nothing—and long to go back to the old days when a man's profit and salary were his own. They are generally honest, thrifty, shrewd, let themselves be governed by precedents and proverbs, and loyally make the sacrifices which are imposed on them.

The Contemporary Generation works in air-conditioned offices, partitioned by flimsy papier-mâché walls, with brittle plywood doors, fluorescent lights, armchairs covered with gay colored plastics. They go in for great allegorical murals in the entrance halls and own no spittoons. Their buildings either have no windows or are all windows. It is the style of the new State Department and of all airport terminals. The Contemporary Generation help themselves in shops and restaurants, easily forming queues with trays in their hands, waiting for food to be slapped on their dishes by an attendant. They are tortured by scruples. They believe in state intervention, in social justice, the future of the United Nations, the possibility of improving mankind with money. They do without servants without grumbling, live simply and are greatly disturbed by the course of human events. They have had to face too many terrifying problems since 1930, the crisis, the totalitarian aggressions, the World War, the postwar years and the Korean War, to be able to draw stable conclusions from their experiences; still they plod ahead with courage, optimism and the will to experiment.

The New Generation has not tasted power yet. They cannot conceive of a life different from the one they have always lived, and they do not wish to see an easier one. They work hard with patience and resignation, without the hope of becoming rich which sustained their grandfathers, and find happiness in being useful and in doing things they consider worthy. They are dressed mostly in shabby clothes. They live in tiny houses or flats, in which they keep their few things in order themselves like sailors on board. Even the rich bachelors often cook their own meals, wash dishes and brush their clothes. The idea of having another citizen of their country or another human being serving them is repugnant to them. Their life promises nothing heroic, glamorous or glorious. They always try to see, to understand, to reason, to go back beyond two wars to the fundamental reasons that made their country wise, prosperous and happy. They are not religious but would like to be, admiring and respecting those who are. They have fully accepted the weight of American responsibilities as an inevitable moral duty.

This is the face of the three Generations. The dividing line does not run along political divisions. The old may be Taft or Truman men; there are progressive dreamers in both parties; whether on the left or right politically, younger people are all preoccupied by the same problems. European observers are tempted to compare these three aspects of American life to three similar waves in European history: for example, to the English conservatives of the early nineteenth century, followed by the reforming liberals, and finally by the prim and virtuous Victorians; or to the laissez-faire conservatives of Louis Philippe, followed by the 1848 Radicals, and finally by the *petit bourgeois* of the Second Empire. All comparisons are misleading, and none can be used as a guide to the future, because the old, the contemporary, and the young Americans are above all Americans, born in their own country, nourished with the ideas, the hopes, the rhetoric and the traditions of America.

*In Europe, you must rub the match against the wall to light it. In America you hold the match to the wall and the wall shakes.*    OLD ITALIAN PEASANT LEGEND

THE TWO GREAT EMPIRES which press Europe from both east and west have this frightening characteristic in common: both are, on paper, philosophical experiments. What Russian life is really like under the Marxist façade and how much of the Old Russia really survives, nobody knows. How intimately American life embodies official hopes and principles is a matter for debate. However, what Europeans know of the United States is the external image, the America of Americans' official descriptions, made up of state papers, pronouncements, policies, the speeches of its statesmen, the movies, the United States Information Service pamphlets, and the Voice of America broadcasts. Similarly, what little they know of Russia is what they learn from newspapers and the proclamations of Communist Party members, the official picture.

Both empires seem obliged to constrict reality within the narrow beds of venerated ideologies; both are surprised, irritated, offended when their efforts to improve

the fate of humanity are unwelcome or when the nature
of men and things escapes from their prefabricated
schemes. Above all, both apparently believe that their
particular way of life will inescapably spread to all men
everywhere and both grimly shoulder the historic duty
of extending at all cost the benefits of their truths to
the rest of the world. The fact that the official philosophy of the United States is more pleasant, acceptable,
and nearer to many Europeans' conception of a desirable
life and the fact, also, that it has represented at least
three times in two centuries the only hope for common
salvation, must not blind Europeans to its bookish, artificial and often unreal quality.

As the Papal Nuncios wear the ancient vestments of
their faith, it would be fitting for the Soviet representatives, on ceremonial occasions, to put on the seedy frock
coat, the steel-rimmed glasses, and the bushy beard of a
Bloomsbury revolutionist of Dickens' time, and for the
American ambassador to wear the homely homespun
clothes, the knee breeches and stockings, the unpow-
dered hair, and the three-cornered hat of their Revolutionary ancestors. The Russians' message is the reverber-
ation of 1848 curses against Manchester capitalists. The
Americans' is the echo of 1790 hopes. The only ills they
clearly distinguish are the eighteenth century's. The
cures they propose are almost always those dear to the
Age of Light. In a way, American representatives often
betray their philosophical age. Official pronouncements
have a taste of Monticello, and their solemn style follows
that of the Founding Fathers. Official stationery is em-

bossed with an eagle and shield which could have been designed by the Adams brothers, and the American flag, as has already been pointed out, is strictly Louis XVI, with the white and red stripes of silk waistcoats and up-holstery, and the stars which were fashionable decorations of the period.

There have been many hopeful revolutions all over the world and most of them have left fundamental things unchanged. Older countries carried on theirs like the impecunious lady who, having inherited a decrepit house with quantities of old furniture, renovates the interior decoration: she shifts a few pieces about, buys new curtains and paints the walls. The Russians and the Americans were the only people able to construct uniform and logical structures, officially shaped according to the founders' ideals. The Russians fought a very feeble *ancien régime*, blew up the house, and exterminated all dissenters. The Americans had few dissenters to deal with, and most of them left the country. The founding of the Republic was practically carried out under ideal conditions, *in vitro*, in a distant, new, unreachable land, where for a long time people had gathered belonging largely to the same class, dedicated to the same beliefs and hopes which were easily turned into noble truths valid for all men and all ages. In older countries ancient traditions, faiths and social classes which had gone out of fashion, were stored in the attic and resurrected when the need came. Institutions hibernated and were later revived as rallying points of "reaction" or the return to "saner views." Some habits always proved themselves stronger than the new laws. Russia and the United States built anew from the foundations, bought all the new furniture, and both claim to have no ideological attic.

Of course, no revolution starts as a philosophical enterprise. The first heroes only vaguely know what they are doing, where they are going, and why. Some of them are always later revolted by their own creation. Officers of the American Army toasted the health of King George III as late as January, 1776. The early American Revolutionists honestly thought they were British Whigs. Only later, philosophers, journalists and pamphleteers explained the Revolution to the rebels and the course of events was then consciously shaped by doctrines.

The doctrines are not pulled out of the sky: they are usually the distillation of common beliefs and hopes. Some are thought to be ancient. Thomas Jefferson wrote that he tried "not to find out new principles, or new arguments, never before thought of" for the Declaration of Independence, but "to place before mankind the common sense of the subject, in terms so plain and firm as to command their assent." *Common Sense* was the title of Tom Paine's pamphlet which supplied Americans with their first vigorous arguments against the ancient world. The power of documents over events grows as the years pass. The heirs consider their heirlooms with increasing veneration, complex motives become simplified, ideas are reduced to the rank of proverbs. In perspective, the early heroes become mythical personalities, all endowed with uniform wisdom, all of one idea and one persuasion. History becomes schoolbook clichés, and schoolbook clichés, imbedded in the younger generations, shape later history. The work is tedious and hard. "Democracy," said Franklin Roosevelt, "is not a static thing, it is an everlasting march." The revolution must go on. Sometimes it is even necessary, as in Russia, to silence or kill the revolutionaries, unable as they often are to understand their early work and to fit into the orthodox pattern. However, in the end, the country begins to look like what it pretends to be, to be permeated by its official ideals. And this is perhaps why the United States looks today even more an eighteenth-century monument than it did in the eighteenth century.

Many contemporaries knew they were witnessing the birth of a nation thoroughly based on their philosophical discoveries. "The idol of the day in Paris," says Imbert de St. Amand, "was Franklin, the peasant, the septuagenarian philosopher, the learned democrat, the man of the future." Even physically the ambassador from the Confederation was the embodiment of the current intellectual fashion, showing his baldness instead of hiding it under a powdered wig, carrying a stick and not a sword, wearing the woollen clothes of the laborer and not the silks of the courtier. Marie Antoinette called him, *"Notre cher républicain."* When he was kissed by Voltaire on both cheeks at the Académie des Sciences somebody wrote, "How beautiful it was to see Solon and Sophocles embracing!"

"The philanthropists, the apologists of perpetual peace demanded war with loud cries. Louis XVI allowed himself to be won over. The apartments of Versailles were filled with solicitors of peril and glory. What transport, what madness, what valor in those paladin philosophers, those chivalrous democrats, having the double passion of glory and liberty, full of superb illusions, of generous follies, and so eloquent, so amiable, so brave! With what gaiety they quitted their pleasures, their châteaux, their theaters to live the life of a soldier!" wrote St. Amand.

Robert Jacques Turgot wrote his friend Doctor Price: "This people is the hope of the human race. It may become the model. It ought to show the world by facts that men can be free and yet peaceful and may dispense with the chains in which tyrants and knaves of every color have presumed to bind them under the pretext of public good. The Americans should be an example of political, religious, commercial, and industrial liberty. The asylum they offer to the oppressed of every nation, the avenue of escape they open, will compel governments to be just and enlightened; and the rest of the world in due time will see through the empty illusions in which policy is conceived."

The Americans themselves were conscious of their historic mission. "I shall not die," Jefferson wrote, "without a hope that light and liberty are on a steady advance. We have seen indeed, once within the record of history, the complete eclipse of the human mind continuing for centuries . . . even should the cloud of barbarism and despotism again obscure the science and liberties of Europe, this country remains to preserve and restore light and liberty to them. In short, the flames kindled on the

4th of July, 1776, have spread over too much of the globe to be extinguished by the feeble engines of despotism; on the contrary, they will consume these engines and all who work for them."

More soberly George Washington wrote, "The American Revolution, or the Peculiar Light of the Age, seems to have opened the eyes of every Nation in Europe."

Whether it was the American Revolution or the Peculiar Light of the Age or both, whether English and French Philosophers had opened the Americans' eyes or whether the American Rebels' shining example had given meaning and force to noble but academic disquisitions, all these are idle questions. It was the Age of Light and Revolution. The same ideas were born at the same time in the heads of men thousands of miles distant, as peach blossoms appear on the same spring day almost everywhere. People were seeking relief from the same problems in Europe and in America, some by writing treatises, others by taking up arms. Everybody was swayed by the same forces, the British fighting their half-hearted battle, as well as the American heroic volunteers, Louis XVI indebting himself and determining his ultimate ruin in order to found the first philosophical republic of the age, as well as the republican noblemen who crossed the ocean to fight tyranny.

Jefferson denied having been influenced directly by those French authors whose ideas could be found in the Declaration of Independence. He had only remembered Lord Kames and John Locke, he said. But Locke had spoken of "life, liberty, and estate," and Jefferson had pulled out of the contemporary air "the pursuit of happiness" which was entirely new. His countrymen, he felt, believed that a government was responsible, if not for happiness, at least for the conditions in which men could pursue it. And what was happiness for an eighteenth-century man? Jefferson and many of his American contemporaries thought at first they were going back to sound principles of English law which the king had violated. Later they recognized they had made the first breach in the century-old wall of tradition; they had revolted against the tranquil acceptance of authority; and they had proudly abandoned the road which had been marked by the passage of generations before them. When Franklin (who believed in little more than God) suggested that the Constitutional Convention open their meeting with prayer, Alexander Hamilton replied, "We're not in need of foreign aid."

In fact, Americans were proud of having found the key to open the gates of man's prison. The key was "common sense." The concluding chapters of Paine's *Rights of Man* contained an outline of political economy that embraced universal education, the abolition of poverty, a reform of the criminal law, pensions for the aged, the reduction of armaments, and international peace. Benjamin Franklin never tired of proposing new plans, some of them useful: a plan for uniting the American colonies, a plan for the abolition of slavery and piracy, a plan for bringing the comforts of civilization to the natives of New Zealand, a plan for a "United Party for

Virtue," organized internationally, a plan for a civil militia, a plan for transforming debts into a philanthropy, a society for the promotion of science and a plan for conversion of the masses to Christianity. A fervid letter to his friend, the English chemist Joseph Priestley, reads, "It is impossible to imagine the height to which may be carried in a thousand years the power of man over matter. We may perhaps learn to deprive large masses of their gravity and give them absolute levity for the sake of easy transport. Agriculture may diminish its labor and double its produce; all diseases may by sure means be prevented or cured, not excepting that of old age, and our lives lengthened at leisure beyond the antediluvian standards. O that moral science were in a fair way of improvement, that men would cease to be wolves to one another, and that human beings would at length learn what they now improperly call humanity."

Like the Japanese wooden pellets which, when dropped in a glass of water, open up into large, complicated and unexpected flowers, the early United States contained, compressed, the history of the next two centuries. Franklin's letter is one of the many examples one may pick up at random. It foresees freight transport by air, the mechanization of agriculture, the improvements of medical science, and yet it stops perplexed in front of what is still the great American stumbling block, the application of scientific technique to the soul of man. The progress of generations never deviated from the plotted course because all final conclusions were logical developments and deductions from original premises which never changed. Why they never changed, Europeans, ignorant as they are of American history, do not know.

They probably never changed because of the Americans' peculiar dislike of abstract thinking, because they were always tacitly considered part of nature's truths, because they appeared to function, and because history never bothered to contradict them for more than a century. They probably never changed also because they were flattering and comfortable explanations of America's successful progress. Readers of Franklin's life could go on believing, for instance, that he had become an important printer because of his shrewdness, his thrift, his ingenuity, his initiatives—in short, for all his traditional virtues—without giving too much weight to the fact that there were no good printers in Philadelphia when he got there. Horatio Alger's legends could be believed in a growing nation busy opening up new territories, founding industries and building new cities where a great number of men, many of them virtuous and obscure, were promoted continuously to commanding positions, but were ironical fables in some European countries, overpopulated and without colonial empires, where the intense and ruthless competition for existence gave success more often to the unscrupulous and the cynical than to the noble and the gentlemanly. The almost-smooth working of democratic institutions, which everybody recognized as an enviable achievement, was also due to the lack of dangerous conflicts in an abundant world and not only to the magic of written statutes, the moderation of statesmen and the functioning of nature's laws. The outbreak of the bloodiest civil war ever fought by civilized men over the first fundamental clash of interests to arise in the United States should have proved the point. Likewise, as America's peace was not protected only by Washington's "Farewell Address" but also by the British Fleet and the balance of power, many Americans never really knew why they had to fight foreign wars whenever British power was challenged, and why they have to defend the whole Western world now that the British have little power left.

It is still called "The Great American Dream" by contemporary writers, this noble and somewhat sacrilegious hope, inherited from the Age of Light, that human intelligence and industry are sufficient to improve man's lot on earth and that no problem exists which cannot be solved. It justifies every contemporary American political decision, like the Marshall Plan and the Point Four Program, it can be read in every major American speech, and it travels over the air waves to warm the heart of listeners all over the world. In his last radio address as President, Harry Truman described it. "With patience and courage we shall some day move on into a new era—a wonderful golden age—an era when we can use the peaceful tools that science has forged for us to do away with poverty and human misery everywhere," he said. "Think what can be done, once our capital, our skills, our science—most of all our atomic energy—can be released from the tasks of defense and turned wholly to peaceful purposes all around the world. There is no end to what can be done. I can't help but dream out loud a little here. The Tigris and the Euphrates Valley can be made to bloom as it did in the times of Babylon and Nineveh. Israel can be made the country of milk and honey as it was in the times of Joshua. There is a plateau in Ethiopia some six to eight thousand feet high, that has sixty-five thousand square miles of land just exactly like the corn belt of Northern Illinois. Enough food can be raised there to feed a hundred million people. These things can be done and they are self-liquidating projects. If we can get peace and safety in the world under the United Nations, the developments will come so fast we will not recognize the world in which we now live."

There is, in these words, the old faith that some day scientific knowledge can bring man back to the Garden of Eden and can wipe out his original sin. (The religious significance is unconsciously brought out by Mr. Truman's words "milk and honey" and his choice of the deserts he wants to see blooming. The Queen of Sheba, it must be remembered, came from Ethiopia.) There is also the practical man's diffidence about financing dreams ("they are self-liquidating projects") and the American's innate trust in contracts, constitutions, covenants, pacts, documents, regulations and institutions ("peace and safety under the United Nations") rather than in his own virtues.

There is nothing wrong with the Great American Dream and American civic ideals except the easy diagnosis of the world's ills and the excessive claims. Nobody in the Western world has doubts about the advantages of liberty and the rule of law. Most of us, especially those who lived under totalitarian regimes, would rather die fighting than accept slavery. It is a convenient choice. Nobody likes hunger, disease, illiteracy. Modern science has undoubtedly made life easier for many. Old fears and miseries which have tormented humanity for centuries have been defeated. Nobody wants to see them back. It is, however, a dangerous illusion to think the devil can be conquered by mere scientists, by well-financed foundations or by research teams. The world is a much worse place and man a much more wicked animal than Mr. Truman or Benjamin Franklin imagine. Progress lets us forget some of the old problems and leaves us with terrible new ones. The dream raises too many hopes among simple people, who are embittered by their continuous failure to reach the promised paradise and by the horror of the strange new world which their efforts seem to bring about. Mr. Truman should probably be grateful not to see the day when the Tigris and Euphrates Valley will bloom.

Twenty years ago an old gentleman, with white piping on his black waistcoat and the large white moustache of a German cavalry officer, sadly tried to explain to me how Americans functioned, while he drank milk and munched biscuits at his Wall Street office desk. We were speaking of Prohibition. "We," he said—embracing all men born on the European Continent, including me and him, Otto Kahn, who was born and had been brought up in the Roman imperial city of Frankfurt—"we always try to imagine what may be the consequences of our acts. Not the Americans. No, they want to try it and see what happens. When they make a mistake they quickly shift course. It is a beautiful but costly and dangerous system."

Americans have always described themselves as the great experimenters, practical people, never ready to accept precedents, dogmas, philosophies, rules of conduct, but who are always trying to discover a new way. The heroes dearest to their hearts are the inventors, the men who bettered the world and opened the way to a "fuller life." Benjamin Franklin invented the stove and the lightning rod. Thomas Jefferson invented a new hemp beater, a new moldboard plow of least resistance, a leather buggy top, a swivel chair, a dumbwaiter, new architectural forms, sent to Naples for the metal molds with which to make macaroni in the United States, and experimented with new fruit trees. Thomas Paine invented a new iron bridge. Samuel Morse, the portrait painter, invented the telegraph. The thought that somewhere, still unknown, an inventor is obscurely at work has always warmed the American heart. Unknown, but perhaps on the threshold of the great discovery which is to give him wealth and fame, like Charles Goodyear that evening when, despairing and having spent his last dollar, he forgot rubber and sulphur on a hot stove. Unknown but at the end of a long and fruitful research, sustained by his faith in his ideas, like Alexander Graham Bell when he spoke in his primitive telephone to his aide in the other room, or like Thomas Edison who said "Mary had a little lamb" into the first gramophone. Unknown, but perhaps already in possession of a machine which will change the face of the world, like the Wright brothers, that September 17, when they wired their sister in Dayton that they had made five successful flights and would be back for Christmas. The inventor is the future and only the future counts. "I'm interested in the future," said Charles Franklin Kettering once. "I'm spending the rest of my life in it."

The last great living American inventor is Charles Franklin Kettering, who invented the electric cash register, the automobile battery ignition system, the self-starter, anti-knock gasoline, a two-cycle Diesel engine and many other devices and processes. He is the nearest thing to a technological saint. Mr. Kettering had been invited, recently, in Chicago, to address a dinner of the American Automobile Engineers. I went with a friend. The inventor was waiting before the dinner in a little room near the banquet hall where all the distinguished guests were drinking cocktails. Mr. Kettering was not drinking. All the men wore their names and their firms' printed on cardboard labels covered with cellophane and pinned to their lapels. Mr. Kettering wore none. Surrounded by admiring younger engineers he stood, waiting, very tall, lean, tired, pale and stooped like all tall men who are hard of hearing and have to lower their heads to hear. He was bald, with a strange hump on top of his shining head. His ears were large and protruding, his lips full and fleshy. His dark clothes, his silence, gravity, patience and obvious authority made him look like a Protestant bishop, the depository of superhuman truths, absorbed by great thoughts and responsibilities.

Mr. Kettering has often repeated, "I call the present time Opportunities Unlimited." He is an optimist. He believes we have barely grazed the mysteries of nature and that much work is still to be done by willing young men. "We worry too much about politics," he once said, "about war, about what men will do who live far away in other continents, when we should really worry about carrying on the work of our fathers." When he was young, he recalled in his after-dinner speech, people used to say: "If we keep on building wooden fences in this country we'll destroy the woods before all the fences are up." Now, he pointed out, the fences are made of steel wire and the woods are still there. When he was young, people worried that the population was growing much faster than food production. The invention of the automobile and the tractor has done away with at least eighteen million mules and horses, he pointed out. And as each mule or horse ate as much as four human beings, the United States can now feed, on the old acreage, about seventy million more inhabitants.

"The road ahead of us," said Mr. Kettering, "is endless." This, in short, is his creed.

Like most of the great figures in American history, he was born on a farm. He can milk a cow and plow a straight furrow. He taught school while studying at Ohio State University until he had to stop when his eyesight failed. He then worked outdoors for the new telephone company to build lines in the country, and he started inventing small devices to make his work easier and more precise. When his eyes improved, he went back to the university where three years later he got his degree. The legend is that he burned the diploma saying, "School does not end here but goes on through life." It is the paraphrase of an old Latin saying, for one of the disadvantages of living in new and empirical countries is that one is often forced to invent old and well-known proverbs. He soon got a job with the National Cash Register Company and quickly invented the O.K. Phone Charge System. Later, he applied an electric motor to the cash register. In 1909 he founded his own firm, the "Dayton Engineering Laboratories," Delco, put the first battery on a car and sold the idea to the Cadillac people.

Mr. Kettering's life closely follows the pattern of the American legend, the ideal of the Age of Light. Born poor (like Rockefeller, Lincoln, Carnegie, Ford, Al Smith, and almost all others), on a farm (like most Presidents, great statesmen and famous writers), handicapped by a serious physical weakness (Edison was deaf, Theodore Roosevelt almost blind, Franklin Roose-

velt had had polio), began life as a common worker
(like Andrew Jackson, Herbert Hoover and so many
others in American life that the list would fill this
book), made his way trusting his own independent genius, applying not abstruse scientific theories (there is
something almost undemocratic and un-American about
difficult theories, which can be understood only by a
handful of expensively trained men, but not by the
boy from the farm) but (like Benjamin Franklin and
Thomas Edison) plain "common sense." "Common
sense," of course, the magic word which recurs through
American history, may also mean the sense of the common people, the ordinary, unrefined, plain, anonymous
people. I have heard people say that acting, playwriting,
movies, strategy, politics, or any other baffling branch of
human activity "is only common sense." Some of them
believed it, I think, and others only hoped it was true.)
Following the national ideal, he dedicated himself to
practical projects, to make life easier to many, and
became extremely rich. His success was not due to
intrigue, the aid of powerful men, or the skillful use of
financial knowledge. It was almost forced on him, who
thought only of his inventions and the good of humanity. This analysis of Mr. Kettering's career is based, naturally, on all the pamphlets, publicity releases, biogra-
phies, magazine articles I could read about him, and not
on a profound study of his real life. Obviously whatever happened to him, as it must have, which did not
coincide with the official pattern his biographers and

probably himself never considered worth-while remembering.

The self-starter was invented in 1910. In the first months of the year a good friend of Mr. Henry Leland, Cadillac's general manager, died as a result of having broken his jaw while cranking his car. Mr. Leland's grief moved the inventor, who started thinking about a device to start a car without using human strength. The problem was a simple one for the man who had already applied an electric motor to turn the cash register's inner mechanisms. On December 17 the first self-starter functioned in the Delco shop. In February the car with the new mechanism was sent to Detroit. Mr. Kettering was at the time in bed with a broken leg: he had met with an accident while testing a new and revolutionary automobile. The car had just arrived when the garage where it was kept burned down. The only existing example of the new invention was destroyed. A new one was immediately built and shipped but, for some reason, did not work. Experiments were to be abandoned and the self-starter considered premature and impractical when, one stormy night, defying the howling wind, the extreme cold, and the snow, without listening to his doctor's or his wife's pleadings, Mr. Kettering hobbled out of bed, hurriedly put on some clothes and took the first train to Detroit. In his hands the new machine worked perfectly. The Cadillac people were sold and signed a two-year contract. Kettering was rich. His invention now for the first time allowed unattended women to drive cars and immediately doubled the number of potential buyers.

Mr. Kettering told us in his speech, that night, that any boy can become an inventor provided he has no knowledge of the problems to study and is willing to try any solution. He said, "Throw away the books," which is one of his famous slogans. Years ago a mechanical engineer who worked for him, Thomas Midgely, having finished some work assigned to him, reported for a new job. Mr. Kettering said, "Go to the laboratory, where you'll find an old wooden box. Inside there are a little machine and some old notes about an experiment I started years ago when I was looking for a better automobile fuel." Midgely protested that he was not a chemist.

"Am I a chemist?" asked Mr. Kettering. "I have no use for chemists who think they already know the answers. I want open-minded people." Under the inventor's guidance, Midgely discovered the advantages of lead tetraethyl, which, added to gasoline, did away with knocking and improved the efficiency of internal combustion engines.

The following story Mr. Kettering often tells to younger men, and he told it after dinner that night. "A friend of mine asked me, years ago, whether it was true that I went from Detroit to Dayton in four and a half hours without speeding. He was the better driver and the trip always took him one more hour. I said it was true and asked him to follow me the following Saturday when I was going home. This he did and we arrived in Dayton in four and a half hours without having passed the speed limit. My friend was mad when we got there.

'You didn't take road 25,' he said. Naturally, I had taken a shorter route which I had worked out on the map. I answered that whoever wants to get somewhere fast should never take road 25 but always a road of his own choosing. And that's the moral of my story."

A Swiss engineer recently visited Mr. Kettering's laboratory in Detroit where the inventor was developing the best possible Diesel engine pistons by testing all possible combinations of metals in actual working conditions. "These pistons," said the European of the model finally chosen, "cannot work." "How do you know?" asked Mr. Kettering. "I'm an engineer," said the other man, "and I can see it." "You may be an engineer," said Mr. Kettering, "but you have never been a Diesel engine piston." One of his favorite sayings is "Let the job be your boss." That evening, in Chicago, after having told some of his favorite stories, he also said this: "It's easy to build a philosophy. It doesn't have to run."

Mr. Kettering often repeats that "Pessimists say things are getting difficult, life runs too fast, and too many problems without solution are piling up. Many think we ought to stop or slow down. An eminent American scholar recently said, 'I'm afraid that too many imbecilic scientists are ruining the world.' I answer, 'Those who think the world is going too fast know where they can go.'"

His is, of course, not a valid answer, because undoubtedly the world is going too fast, and many people believe that machines must be easy to build if Mr. Kettering's open-minded farm boys can build them. But philosophies must be difficult to keep functioning, to adapt, repair, make useful and comforting to contemporary man, if Mr. Kettering, who drives around in his latest automobile and hops about the country in his up-to-the-minute private plane, is still using Benjamin Franklin's philosophy, which is obviously inadequate today.

The inventor's real dream is an ambitious one. In 1925, head of the research division of General Motors, enriched by his many patents, a successful man, Mr. Kettering decided to tackle a really difficult job, something more important than the self-starter or the O.K. Phone Charge System, something that would really change the life of man on the earth. He tackled it with his usual tools, open-minded experimenting, and common sense. He set out to discover and reproduce the process by which plants absorb and transform solar energy into chemical energy, or, as he puts it, "why the grass is green."

He said, at about that time, "All the existing coal and oil reserves are the equivalent of five weeks of solar energy. All energy comes from the sun. It is the sun that lifts water to such heights that it can move turbines on the way down, generating electric current. It is the sun that created coal and oil in the remote past and it is the sun that moves internal combustion and steam engines. But between us and the sun there is a mystery. How do plants transform heat and light into energy? Why is grass green?"

His personal experimenting was insufficient for such a large operation and he subdivided it into separate tasks, assigning them to separate research groups all over the country. He merely gathered the results, controlled the experiments in his own laboratories, and co-ordinated the whole project. Important discoveries were made on the chemical formation of plants, which opened up new paths for research on their behavior under different laboratory conditions, on their growth in the absence of light and of various specific chemicals, which again gave rise to new theories, some of which proved themselves useful in agriculture. The years passed. Libraries were filled with the meticulous compilations of scientists. Mr. Kettering's aides detected and followed all sorts of different trends in the secret conduct of algae, but the solution of the original mystery is still as far away as it was in 1925. Why is grass green?

I asked Mr. Kettering, before dinner, how his work on solar energy was getting on. "We got the problem in a corner," he said tiredly. "It can't get away from us." With a sullen and tired voice, he was repeating a stock answer, the sort of cheerful answer he probably was famous for many years before, when he tackled less complicated jobs and always came up with a solution. His voice was barely audible in the noise of the small cocktail room. "We are on the right road," he said.

Did the old inventor now know he was going to die without having discovered the ultimate secret of nature? Did he suspect that we have reached the point when diligence, the piling up of experimental results, the co-ordination of statistics, the abundance of technical facilities, and common sense are no longer enough?

The large and dramatic advertisement in the morning paper, months ago, was signed "Sinclair—A Great Name in Oil" and was topped by two pictures. One showed an eighteenth-century, shirt-sleeved mechanic leisurely working at his bench, probably filing a cog wheel. The caption explained, "In 1793 Eli Whitney built his cotton gin in a barnyard—with his own hands and homemade tools—and it worked. For then technology was simple, and a man could prove out his invention on his own. In contrast, the recent development of nylon took ten years of research time and seventy millions of dollars." Under the second picture, showing two frock-coated gentlemen talking with dignified excitement, were the words, "In 1876 Alexander Graham Bell had nothing but an idea, a few dollars' worth of materials, and an attic workshop. Yet he built and proved the first telephone. Today, however, great laboratories are needed to prove a new idea in communications—facilities which are unavailable to most independent inventors."

Then came a generous proposal in large type: "An Offer of Research Facilities to Inventive Americans Who Need Them." The text explained, "Inventive

Americans are often at a loss today. Not because of any lack of ideas, but because of a need for large and expensive facilities to find out if and how their ideas work. This was no obstacle in our earlier days. The Wright brothers designed their first airplane with the help of a foot-square, homemade 'wind box'—and the plane flew. In contrast the man with a new idea in airplane design today often needs a supersonic wind tunnel costing millions. In short, science and invention have become so complex that a man with an idea often needs the assistance of many specialists and millions' worth of equipment to prove his idea has value." Then came the new offer. "Within the petroleum field, the Sinclair Plan now offers to provide that assistance. Under this Plan, Sinclair is opening up its great research laboratories at Harvey, Illinois, to independent inventors who have sufficiently good ideas for better petroleum products or for new applications." The technical details of the Plan followed.

Obviously, the Sinclair Oil Company directors were aware that something had changed in the contemporary world. The unknown farm boys perhaps came up with fewer inventions or the inventions they made only changed the surface of life and revolutionized a few technical details but left fundamental things substantially intact. Was this the end of the road? The meaning of American life has always been eternal change, improvement and renovation. From the new ideas Americans expect relief from old miseries and solutions to ancient problems. Was it true, as Mr. Kettering had said, "that pessimists think things are getting difficult, life runs too fast, and too many problems without a solution are piling up?" The Sinclair Oil Company directors took their brave stand. The trouble, they said, was that not enough inventions were being made. Inventive Americans had always been able to give an answer to most of the world's riddles but were often "at a loss to-day" for lack of "large and expensive facilities." What they needed was a carefully worded Plan, a covenant between them and Powerful Financial Interests. What they needed was more and more money, more and more laboratory space, more and more time to pursue their ideas. Only then would the flow of important and revolutionary discoveries start again.

After so many years in Europe, I had forgotten how close America had come to realizing the dream of the Founding Fathers, how incredible were her power and wealth created by her ancient faith in experiments and inventions and her honest hope to better man's lot on earth. One early morning, at a military base in Georgia, as I witnessed swarm after swarm of planes drop thousands of parachutists who filled the sky as jellyfish fill the Mediterranean on some windless days, guns, trucks, and packing cases of food and ammunition as big as railroad cars, and as I saw all this floating gently to the ground (the parachutes were all of different color to distinguish their loads), I thought of Doctor Franklin's words, "We may perhaps learn to deprive large masses of their gravity for the sake of easy transport."

On my last trip, I saw the American scene again with the bewildered eyes of the European, accustomed to the miniature scenery of the Old World. At night America was especially frightening, when you no longer saw the faces of people but looked at the immense landscapes. The long bridges spanning the darkness, over which chains of glowworms traveled slowly, and under which lighted ships floated, like gondolas under the stone bridges of Venice, against the jagged curtain of black skyscrapers, punched with lights; the immense cities, seen from the air, spiderwebs of tiny lights from horizon to horizon, as big as Italian provinces or Tyrrhenian islands, over which the plane crawled laboriously, trying to reach the outskirts; the monstrous factories glowing in the night, the acres of floodlighted railroad yards crowded with thousands of cars, all this awed me. I had forgotten how incredibly rich America was. I looked in wonder at the proud abundance of everything, at the shop windows, at the well-dressed people, at the absence of the poor, at the long queues of shining cars on the roads, waiting for traffic to move, all filled with gay, well-fed, pink people, the parking lots outside factories or stadiums, where all the cars of a medium-sized European country could be parked. I had also forgotten all the conveniences of America, the large and warm libraries where any book could be easily found, the spotless hospitals, the symphonic orchestras maintained by public subscription, the great drives for welfare funds, the wealthy universities whose prosperous teachers looked not at all like their hungry European colleagues but like businessmen. Above all, I rediscovered the principal pleasure of life in America, which is the absence of fear, diffidence, suspicion and envy—all of which makes relations with Americans always easy and friendly. I had also forgotten how lucky American children were.

One day I happened to spend a few hours on a small farm near Anniston, Alabama. I had to wait there for somebody to pick me up. There was an old wooden house which needed a coat of paint. The old farmer and his wife showed me around. They had three cows, about twenty chickens, two great pecan trees and five acres of land. They would be starving in Europe. Here they apparently were as well off as small shopkeepers. They had an old car in the garage which they wouldn't change as they rarely used it. The house was furnished with coquetry: pretty curtains at the windows, flowers in their pots, gay pillows on the chairs. The old couple had all sorts of conveniences, a radio-and-television set, a washing machine and other machines which I did not recognize.

In the cellar the old lady had put away rows of glass jars with homemade preserves. "I could buy all of them in the store with much less trouble," she said, "but I like doing my own, as I always did. It keeps me busy." They showed me pictures of two sons, one in his Army uniform in Korea, the other a clerk somewhere in a big city, and she told me how well they were doing. The old man did not bother to keep a vegetable garden. (He said he did, but it amounted to a row of sickly cabbages that the chickens had devastated long before.) "I could do a lot more work," he said, "but I'm old and we don't need more than we've got."

The cows came by themselves twice a day to the milk shed to be milked by machinery. The milk was deposited in sterilized cans which were picked up at regular hours by a truck from a dairy. They asked me about Europe, whether there was going to be a war, and whether people there suffered much. I told them about life on a farm like theirs, the olive trees which must be pruned and helped with fertilizer once a year, about the vineyards, the way to make good wine and good oil, how everything is done by hand, except plowing and threshing, how bread is made in an open oven. The old couple nodded, as if they had seen it all or were remembering things from their past. Then the woman asked, "Are people happy over there?"

Of course, an Italian farmer could not afford such a beautifully furnished house with all those machines on the milk of three cows, three calves a year, ten eggs a day, and the nuts from two trees. The Italian farmer had no car, no washing machine, but a much larger vegetable garden, a cellar full of wine, olive oil, hanging chains of onions and garlic, dried figs, and lots of children. Undoubtedly the Italian ate better, worked more and lacked the medical services, the comfortable tools, the professional assistance the old couple had. Are people happy in Europe?

When I left, the old couple gave me a pocketful of pe-
cans to sow in my garden in Rome. "You'll remember
us all your life looking at the trees," said the woman.
The man said, "Put them in a pot of good earth in the
autumn. It takes them a long time to open."

How far the United States is from achieving its dream
is told by American newspapers every day.

The picture one gets from the daily news is one of
general corruption, dishonesty, decadence, incompe-
tence, decay, such as communists would and often do
gladly reproduce without alterations. We learn that tax
bureau officials can be bought, high-school children take
heroin, dock workers are slaves in the hands of gangsters, Washington bureaucracy is filled with petty
crooks, the political machines of most big cities are in
the hands of criminals, students cheat in their examina-
tions, military transport planes filled with innocent pas-
sengers crash because of the pilot's incapacity and of
the bad design of planes not properly tested, thirteen-
year-old girls are known to sleep with boy friends,
dangerous communist agents hide in the most delicate
federal, industrial and armed forces posts.

American diplomats, we read, are easily deceived by
Germans, Russians, British, French, Chinese, Persians,
Spaniards. The stored wheat on which the Department
of Agriculture advances credits to farmers is sold with

the complicity of crooked officials, Negroes are tossed out of restaurants, schools and jobs because of their color, basketball players sell games to the highest bidder, wrestling matches are fixed. Serious and well-informed newspapers print all this almost every day, with a full documentation of names, cases and authoritative opinions. The more popular press shrieks with delight at the daily discovery of the depths to which human beings can plunge.

Foreigners get an even more sinister picture of American life from current books, in some of which the vices of contemporary society are described in frank and open language such as not even Emile Zola dared to use in his probing of French vices under the Second Empire. A certain lassitude can be detected in most Americans when you turn to them for explanations. They smile bitterly, suggest that what you have read is nothing, that things really are much worse than that, and repeat old slogans with an ironic grimace. "God's Own Country," they say, "It's a free country," or "The Land of the Free and the Home of the Brave" and laugh.

The discovery that they are human beings, after all, like all other human beings, has always shocked Americans. Each one, I believe, knows that he himself is human. Each one hates, loves or is resigned to his foibles, defects, unclean desires, and corrupt nature; but each one perhaps hopes to be only an exception in a world populated predominantly by semi-divine human beings, in a society working generally toward perfection. This is merely a hypothesis, for I found it difficult to get

Americans, except the weak and the drunk, to talk about these things. When, however, they discover that their neighbors are no better than they, they are deeply discouraged.

The feeling is as old as the Federal Union. General Knox wrote in dismay to Washington, after Shays' Rebellion, that "Americans were, after all, men—actual men possessing all the turbulent passions belonging to that animal." All my life I have heard Americans sincerely and bitterly disparaging the United States. Only rarely and self-consciously have they confessed they loved their country because it was the best in the world, the highest achievement in human civilization. At the same time, they resent as a rule a foreigner's confirming their criticisms, and they visibly love being praised and appreciated. All this is frankly puzzling to Europeans, especially to Italians, who seldom claim superhuman wisdom for their country and who are seldom plunged into despair by the discovery that among their countrymen there are crooks, cowards, weaklings or dishonest politicians.

What especially baffles foreigners is this continuous swing from shrill praise to unjustified bitterness, as if the road the American people have traveled seemed to them nothing like the road they still have ahead of them. The road they have traveled looks very impressive to friends and enemies alike. The United States has created the greatest organization for the production and distribution of goods in history. No people has enjoyed better health and kept the old folks alive so long. Here and there democratic organizations may be conquered by crooks, but a healthy fear of public opinion keeps them often in check and the case is not the general rule. More often the machinery of government is in the hands of reasonably honest men. Ideological and personal rivalries are not decided by means of clubbings, nighttime arrests by the secret police, concentration camps or forced labor, but by speeches, often dull, debates, press conferences and ballots. There are more schools, universities, colleges, educational institutions, welfare organizations, orchestras, dramatic societies, garden clubs, hospitals, clinics and libraries in the United States than in all the rest of the globe.

It matters little if the suburban ladies who listen to an afternoon lecture on art may be ridiculous in their appreciation of third-hand knowledge, or if the rendition of *Hamlet* by an amateur dramatic society may be considered humorous by experts. What really matters is that ladies are turning their thoughts to art in great numbers and that clerks dedicate their free evenings to the study of dramatics. Americans fought two world wars without asking for anything in return. They blanketed the rest of the world in the two postwar periods with wheat, medicines, old clothes, raw materials, cotton and coal, without anybody thanking them for their trouble. They helped save the lives of millions—mostly the very young and the very old—and saved many nations from collapse and revolution, with no other thought than the hope to enjoy their share of the common peace after it was re-established.

This side of America, the honest, Christian, provincial country, ready to offer help and to relieve suffering, is perhaps more impressive than the majestic cities, the mighty skyscrapers, the immense factories. You see it clearly from the air, when the plane crosses farming country: a carpet of farms, each with its freshly painted house, surrounded by a little flower garden and a few trees, the silo, the stable, the barn, a car parked in the drive, a tractor at work somewhere, all farms more or less alike, from horizon to horizon. The compact pattern of cultivated fields looks like a gigantic enlargement of living tissue seen through a microscope—which is what it really is, living tissue of the American body, source of its strength.

Europeans do not usually understand that Americans are not really disgusted with their country, not even the expatriates who seek a better climate for their art, their dreams or their snobbishness. Their feeling about things as they are in the United States is the irritation of the man who has dropped a penny in the slot machine and did not get either his chewing gum or his money back. He believes in the machine. He fumes, shakes, punches, and curses it because, in his view of the universe, it is inconceivable for an automatic distributor not to deliver the goods after it has been paid. The discovery that it, too, can make mistakes and cheat him destroys his inner peace.

Similarly, Americans have inherited from their past the belief that life, too, in spite of everything, can be made to function like a machine. If you put the right amount of money in the right place—millions in the hands of specialized scientists, for instance—if you carry on the correct experiments, if you follow the technical instructions printed on the box, if you sign carefully worded contracts, you must always get satisfactory results. When history does not deliver the gum, when things are not as they should be, when injustice prevails, when failure crowns your efforts, when, in spite of all hopes, man shows himself as he has always been, Americans are eternally surprised and maddened—more so than any other people, perhaps, because they are defenseless. "How can things be as they are," they seem to say, "after we have devised the wisest political statutes, we have endowed the masses with universal education, we have given them the highest standard of living, through the work of our inventors, industrialists, and scientists, who are the best in the world, we have allowed nothing of the old world to survive, we have taken a new empirical approach to every problem, and we have spared no effort to approach perfection in all fields?" They usually conclude that they are traveling the right road but that the work done is still insufficient. What they need is more experimenting, more inventing, a still greater break from the past, an even more revolutionary approach to the old problems.

# IV

*Put none but Americans on guard tonight.*

GEORGE WASHINGTON

THE ROMANS conquered the world with their roads, their administrators and their soldiers. The Mongols overwhelmed all enemies from Turkestan to Poland because they alone knew how to shoot arrows from galloping horses. The British discovered that whoever dominated the seas ruled the lands.

The Americans inherited Christendom in 1945 because they not only are able to design and build wonderful machines but can also reproduce them in great quantity, at great speed, and at a low cost. Their principal contribution to industrial technique, the source of their monstrous power, has been compared to the invention of printing. Before Gutenberg, of course, there were already philosophical treatises, verses of a few great poets, prayers, histories and holy books, but they were precious documents which few could see. After Gutenberg, wisdom was not increased, but the world was flooded with words, no longer as awe-inspiring as they had been, but free for everyone to read and learn.

This American capacity to bring forth machines with

stupefying fecundity, and not the atomic bomb, saved the peace in the beginning. Pietro Quaroni, one of the shrewdest diplomats in Europe, who was Italian ambassador in Moscow the last year of the war, told me that, as soon as the Russians conquered the first German city destroyed by American bombing raids, work was stopped on the Moscow subway, plans were revised, and new tunnels dug at twice the depth of the old ones. He also tells the story of a meeting between Stalin and an American general. The American praised the heroism of the Red Army, their brave and bloody stand at Stalingrad, their overwhelming offensives in the winter of 1943-44. Stalin nodded and, at every pause in the other man's speech, repeated the same words. "Yes, yes," he said over again, "you're right. But we Russians could not have organized the Normandy landing." The memory of the abundance with which Americans answered the Russians' call for help, the avalanche of machines, weapons, food, raw materials, fuel, petroleum products which was released in a few months, is also responsible for the caution shown until now by the Soviet general staff. Nothing impresses the Russians and the Americans alike more than industrial organization and mass production.

This yearning to produce identical machines in infinite numbers is rooted deep in the American character. Learned essays could be written, without really explaining this phenomenon, on the influence of Calvinism and Puritan thought on industrial organization, on the influence of an empty continent which needed everything on the Americans' ingenuity, on the love of uniformity and standardization in a country in which individualism and diversity could have meant death in the struggle against savages and nature. Many, everywhere, have tried to imitate it by copying American factories and technique. Workers have been meticulously instructed in every gesture; machinery, engineers, and overseers have been imported. Other people often succeeded in designing better machines, in finishing them to a finer perfection. Nobody has yet been able to make so many of them, so fast, with so little effort and expenditure, while paying workers such high salaries. An American I know owns identical factories in Italy and in the United States. He uses the same raw material, which he buys in bulk for both enterprises, produces the same goods with the same process. He pays his American workers several times the Italians' salaries. His Italian goods cost him about four times the American product.

Similar experiments have been tried almost everywhere with similar results. Italians, like most Europeans, love to make few things, one at a time, anything which challenges the single man's ingenuity and skill, and they want to change over to something else when they are finished. There is nothing mysterious about the Americans' production technique except the fact that they love it. They apparently believe in it as the Italians of old believed in building cathedrals, the French in good food, the Germans in philosophy, the Japanese in duty. The sight of other people's inefficiency fills them with dismay, as the sight of good but unused land distresses the Italians.

It took the Americans almost three years—too late to save China and Eastern Europe—before they began to suspect what had happened, that they were alone in the world, that history was to be shaped by their decisions, the decisions of the President, of the Secretary of State, the generals in the Pentagon, the senators and the representatives. From then on Mr. Harry Truman of Independence, Missouri, was to be the successor of Benjamin Disraeli, Gladstone, Richelieu, Charles V; Mr. Dean Acheson was to be their Metternich, Talleyrand, Castlereagh; homely Omar Bradley, the "schoolteacher general," was to fill the shoes of Julius Caesar, von Clausewitz, Napoleon, von Moltke and Wellington. They tackled their job reluctantly and earnestly, with the tools their national history had provided them, with their reliance on "common sense" which had never failed them since Tom Paine's days, their official myths, their old habits, prejudices, illusions, their impatience with things as they are and their certainty in a perfect future. It was a wonderful and terrifying sight to watch them work, doing the right things (because history moves men and nations in spite of themselves) for the wrong motives, save the world, save it from ruin, strengthen it, and defend it. It was a little like watching Mr. Charles F. Kettering, made Emperor of the World, carry on his new duties with his rule-of-thumb technique, his contempt for philosophy, his reliance on experimenting, his belief in the job, and, at the same time, his blind and unconscious acceptance of ancient values, which are part of him, and make him, in the end, do the things he does.

Dean Acheson, of course, was the Charles F. Kettering of international affairs, the man who had to take the most decisions during the fateful years, and who reluctantly and experimentally had to invent American policy to avoid immediate disasters, to save the peace and shape the future. It was difficult to understand why he was disliked by the American public in general. The main accusations against him were two and partly contradictory: he was considered, at the same time, but by different people, a tool of the Kremlin and a stooge of the British Foreign Office. The first critics pointed out that he was one of the *illuminati* who had come to Washington at the time of the Roosevelt revolution, some of whom were *bona fide* communists; that he had had kind words for Alger Hiss; that he had talked General Marshall into rejecting the Pentagon's plan to reinforce Chiang Kai-shek, and into accepting John Carter Vincent's idea: to form a coalition government of Chinese communists, Chiang's men, and a Third Force of Chinese liberals who turned out not to exist. He had been unfortunate enough to say that he was "waiting for the dust to clear" when speaking of his China policy, had advised withdrawal of United States forces from South Korea in 1949, and had given the Soviets the wrong impression when he said, in December, 1949, that nobody could guarantee to protect Formosa and Korea from aggression.

The second group of critics generally charged him with having sacrificed Asia for the sake of Europe and of British interests. In all Middle East emergencies, it was pointed out, the State Department had been caught unprepared and surprised by the turn of events, and hurriedly accepted a ready-made policy from the British Foreign Office as one accepts an old, possibly ill-fitting dry suit from a friend when caught in a shower. British policy was rarely adapted to American needs. It was old-fashioned, designed for a colonial world which disappeared years ago, impractical, imperialistic, ignored new nationalistic feelings and, instead, counted heavily on bribing Cabinet Ministers and behind-the-scenes wire pulling.

All this was in contrast with traditional American ideals and aims, among which the conservation of the British Empire from decay had never been included. Acheson's friends tried to point out that his had been the irregular course of a skipper who makes the best of shifting winds, that he had protected Europe and let Asia go because he had not enough power to do both, and that while the loss of Asia had been a grave defeat, the loss of Europe might have been fatal. In spite of Mr. Truman's own attempt at defending his Secretary of State, the general feeling against him ran so unreasonably high, both among Democrats and Republicans, that observers were puzzled. The real causes must not be the apparent ones, some foreign correspondents concluded: they must be deep, irrational, unconscious.

Perhaps the former Secretary of State was disliked mainly because he reminded Americans of their new foreign policy, their international responsibilities, the Soviet nightmare, the rest of the world to feed and shore up, the atomic bomb, and a military budget proportionate to their new commitments. Perhaps he was disliked because he looked like an "aristocrat" (the word is seldom used in Europe but is frequently found in American popular novels and magazines), or like an Englishman. Undoubtedly, Acheson always tried hard to look and dress like an Englishman. No Englishman is as English as he appears; only a few members of the Paris Jockey Club, Spanish dukes with English relations, and Sicilian landowners manage to equal him, as they all reproduce a model gentleman who vanished many years ago, destroyed by irony, two World Wars, and taxes. Acheson's accent could easily be taken for English by provincial Americans who do not recognize it for what it really is, High Episcopal clergy, Connecticut, Groton, Yale, Harvard and a good law office. When he speaks, he crosses his long legs, first the left over the right and then the right over the left, as many do in the House of Lords, never moves his hands, and uses only the choicest words.

When I saw him, he always repeated carefully

worded generalities: that the United States' aim was peace, that international collaboration should be based on perfect partnership among equals, that Russia must prove with facts and not words her desire for peace, that collective security was the world's great hope. These things he said solemnly, as if he really thought in terms of proclamations and editorials. He was disliked by journalists because he rarely gave them a real story, and because at his press conferences he recognized only one of them by his name, James Reston of the New York *Times*, whom he did not call "Scotty" but always *Mister* Reston. He was impatient with stupid questions, with ignorance, with forgetfulness. His answers were often snappy, ironical, and cutting, such as a gentleman of past generations could have used.

What most Washington people disliked about him was his air of "leave-it-to-papa" and "papa-knows-best." If Acheson had been a character in a drama, or in a nineteenth-century novel, the public would have classified him immediately as he entered the scene, a stiff Tory, attached to the defense of things as they were, including moral values, ancient institutions, the family, the law, religion, the correct seat on a horse, and the art of handling one's inferiors. Acheson's past confirms this picture of him. The son of the Episcopal bishop of Connecticut, strictly brought up in a small Eastern town, educated by an English governess—nothing about his childhood could recall Mark Twain and the simple life of most American boys. Groton, Yale and Harvard kept his

early personality intact—that of a man who could un-
bend only among his social peers and who kept a severe
front for all others.

That was not the character Dean Acheson thought
he was. He saw himself as a Whig, a liberal nurtured by
Felix Frankfurter, who gave him his first job as law
clerk to Justice Brandeis and then suggested his name
to President Roosevelt for a post in the Treasury. He
saw himself as part of the American revolutionary tradition, an American empiricist, who refused to accept
things as immutable. "We must decide nothing in advance," he once said. "There are no final solutions for
all problems. All decisions must come from an analysis
of facts." It is the Kettering illusion. He also said, "In
times of moral and intellectual anarchy, our only guide
must be reason and the spirit of man." It is the Founding
Fathers' faith, the rationalistic creed of the eighteenth
century. Acheson liked to think that there were no fixed
principles. He often repeated one of Justice Brandeis'
favorite sayings: "Man has been created to formulate
general principles, none of which is worth anything."
That problems could be solved day by day with decisions
based on carefully gathered data and that there was no
such thing as a valid general principle ("Let the job be
your boss" and "Philosophies are easy to make: they
don't have to run," says Mr. Kettering) were the hopes
he most frequently expressed, just as a little boy firmly
repeats to himself, "Ghosts don't exist" as he walks into
a dark room.

Dean Acheson was not a happy man. His severe and

ironical manner betrayed his misery. He probably disliked himself as much as his critics did, for the man he tried to be was not the man he was, the world he was compelled to accept and to shape got further and further away from his adolescent hopes and beliefs. Still, he never entirely abandoned his humanitarian dreams for *realpolitik*, and he did not totally adopt Machiavellian expediency against his earlier ideals. He merely tried to do the best he could, torn between two contrary imperatives. This is why Dean Acheson was something more than one of Mr. Truman's Cabinet: for one moment in history, he was the United States.

The State Department is undoubtedly the most impressive depository of information the world has ever seen. In its immense files billions of facts sleep like the unused antiques in the late Mr. William Randolph Hearst's warehouses. All that can be ascertained, measured, weighed, estimated, described, recorded in the political, financial, economic, meteorological, medical, private, public and secret life of any country has been gathered, classified, and filed. There are the mountains of political documents captured from the enemy, the secret findings of agents, the United States embassies' constant flow of reports, European Recovery Program and Point Four technical surveys and data gathered by specialized field teams.

The State Department literally wants to know everything. Foreign journalists are frightened by the minute questions about their country asked them by American officials on the significance of minor speeches by unknown politicians, on the importance of unread pamphlets or editorials and on incidents which went unrecorded in their own press. The State Department is just as eager to distribute information. Requests for data on any topic open a chute over the head of the unsuspecting correspondent; he is literally buried under an avalanche of mimeographed material, most of which is accurate, up to date, ample, exhaustive, but too abundant, simple, and irrelevant for any purpose other than the leisurely preparation of almanacs.

From all this one rarely gets a general idea. The official in charge of country X, for instance, can dig out the age, psychology, and *curriculum vitae* of the Prime Minister, the name of his sweetheart, the average rainfall for the last fifty years, a description of the prevalent diseases, an elaborate analysis of the country's economic plights, and many other facts, but he is rarely ready to answer the only question one wants to ask: "What is the State Department doing in order to keep this country solidly within the sphere of the Atlantic alliance?"

Of course, diplomats never answer broad questions in any country. Evasive answers come naturally to them. Americans of all professions and classes never like to discuss abstract principles. State Department officials speak freely only with American journalists they have known a long time and are extremely careful when talking with foreigners.

All this is true. However, one gets the impression that State Department officials dislike any theoretical question for other reasons. They see themselves as the priests of details, the slaves of their immense deposit of information, too absorbed by the daily flow of paper to formulate theories or to discuss them except in the most simplified terms. Their job is not to distill truth or ideas. These will have to generate themselves somehow like flowers from a mound of refuse. Ideas, sometimes, may be slow in coming, and the same data may produce conflicting theories and suggest contradictory lines of action. There is practically nothing anybody can do about it except to go on with the job in hand. The more things become complicated, dangerous and bewildering, the more additional data on the subject must be gathered. Sometimes one feels that this frenzied search for facts, statistics, news, the creation of new bureaus, staffed with more men, the spending of large sums of money, all this may be the only way Americans know to express their anxiety.

This story is current among State Department foreign correspondents. One day, the Secretary of State sent out a memorandum of two hundred words asking for specific data to prove one particular point—perhaps the danger to European defense of German steel and coal cartels, or the desirability of a plebiscite to settle the Trieste problem between Italy and Yugoslavia. The experts dug into the files and brought out an immense quantity of material which they boiled down to a 400-page report. This was read by higher officials and re-

duced to 100 pages for the Secretary's staff. The 100
pages were then cut to 20 pages for the Secretary's assistant, who prepared a 200 word synopsis of the whole
argument for his boss to read over the week-end. The
ultimate extract was nothing more than a paraphrase
of the original memorandum. The story, of course, is
not true.

The *Pax Americana*, the uneasy peace which Harry
Truman and Dean Acheson saved for all of us and which
Dwight Eisenhower and John Foster Dulles have inherited, is precarious, costly and dangerous. The tranquillity in which we live is that of wrestlers embraced
in a deadly grip, with bulging muscles and bursting veins.
The future looks dangerous. Something will have to
happen. Either war will break out, the war really to
end all wars, all problems, and all humanity, too, or we
must manage somehow to build a more endurable and
less costly peace.

Can Americans do the job, can they lead us to build
a more endurable and less costly peace? They have the
power. Have they the necessary virtues? Up till now,
they have erected beautiful castles in the air, fairy-tale
organizations based on good will, the fundamental de-
cency of all men, and a supposed desire common to all
nations for peace and prosperity. And all emergencies
have come to them as exceptions, storms which would

calm down. They have always been unprepared, surprised, grieved, indignant and brave. We have repeatedly
seen American firemen caught asleep, with no engines,
rush to the fire, putting on their clothes on the way and
improvising fire-fighting techniques of some sort while
machines were made ready for them. We have seen
Americans shore up falling masonry and patch up holes
at great expense. They probably had no time to do anything else.

But we would like to know if they can design a stable
political structure, a house to relax in, a system which
will allow us to help them carry the common burden.
Can they construct the American empire? Or will they
muff their chance in history? Are they too tied to their
prejudices, habits, noble hopes, and past experience to
do the job? Must they always, like good empiricists,
allow the "job to be their boss," which means leaving
the initiative to the outside world, or adopt a passive
attitude and be prepared only to defend themselves? Must
they always learn everything from scratch and always
begin anew?

An old Italian diplomat confessed to me some time
ago, "To tell the truth, I read the newspapers, the tele-
grams, the reports, the political speeches and I understand nothing. Then, slowly, I put away the contemporary jargon, the United Nations, the international ideals
and their terminology, and translate things into the language which Metternich would have used. Only then
can I begin to understand what is really happening, iden-
tify the motives which move the various countries, the

forces in the field, and look to the future." International affairs are now hidden under a heavy mist of noble words and handled by organizations which are a camouflage for the real activity, which is not always noble, but ancient and effective. Reality calls for concrete decisions, based on an exact valuation of forces and intentions. History does not obey words and hopes but power, which may also be spiritual power, when expressed in the determination and will to fight and conquer.

"Take the Korean War," said the Italian diplomat. "It is officially a war carried out by an international organization, the United Nations, against an aggressor. The New York *Times* always speaks of the Western forces as U.N. Army, Navy, Air Force. Technically, it is right. But the reality which Metternich would have understood is another. It is a war carried out by a powerful nation, for reasons of her own, helped by a satellite, the South Koreans, and by a sprinkling of unwilling allies, who sent token forces for political reasons, as weak and reluctant allies sent their meager contingents to join Napoleon's Grande Armée. All you have to do to understand this is to confront real United Nations losses with United States losses. You get the arithmetical proportion between the two wars, the very small one carried out under the blue and white flag and the large one carried out under the Stars and Stripes."

To build an endurable peace, the State Department should perhaps begin to think about problems in the Metternich terminology, without necessarily following the Metternich policies. Will the State Department now, under Republican leadership, forget the verbal inheritance of Woodrow Wilson, Franklin Roosevelt, and Cordell Hull? Cordell Hull, when illustrating the advantages of the United Nations Charter to Congressmen, said, for instance, that there would no longer be need for "spheres of influence, alliances, blocs, balance of power," nor of any of those devices with which, "in the unhappy past, nations have attempted to guarantee their security and promote their interests."

This was in 1945. Cordell Hull's words would not be repeated by any responsible American leader today. Dwight Eisenhower, in his inaugural address, simply called the United Nations "the living sign of all people's hope for peace" and said, "We shall strive to make it not merely an eloquent symbol but an effective force."

Do Americans accept the necessity of "those devices," which are the only ones with which peace has always been defended and the technical means by which any policy, either aggressive and imperialistic, or noble and disinterested, can be promoted? Or do they think of them as a temporary return to barbarous conceptions, a block on the road to progress, something they have been compelled to adopt against their will by the devilish cunning of the Politburo?

Among the convictions which have traditionally shaped American foreign relations are the two following:

—that, under the skin of every inhabitant of the earth, whatever may be his picturesque appearance, his incomprehensible philosophy, or his terrifying attitude, there is really a Middle Western bourgeois hidden away;

—that it is a generally recognized fact that no nation or coalition of nations can ever equal or surpass the United States, to whose wealth, power, technical knowledge no undertaking is impossible.

There is sufficient truth in these two canons for them to have lasted a long time. Nobody doubts that there is something in common between a citizen of Akron, Ohio, Independence, Kansas, or Sioux City, Iowa, and any other human being on the face of the earth, a Kenya Mau-Mau, a Sicilian sulphur miner, a Chinese tea planter, a Greek sponge fisherman: horror of captivity, of slavery, love for the peace in which to enjoy the delights of life, a reasonable passion for wealth and personal power, and so forth. Why is the *Reader's Digest,* a magazine edited exclusively to please Middle Western middle-class readers, the most popular and widely sold publication everywhere in the world? Thus, one frequently hears in the United States the suggestion that the best and quickest way to destroy the power of the Kremlin would be to drop several million copies of the Sears Roebuck catalogue all over Russia. If Russians were, under the skin, the same as the inhabitants of Kansas, they should appreciate in their just value the advantages of so many home appliances at such good prices and be ready to revolt against a regime which deprives them of what Americans consider the bare necessities for human life.

Naturally, as one travels away from the ideal center, the resemblances fade and become blurred. Already on the Atlantic coast of the United States men tend to differentiate themselves from the model, a tendency resented by most Americans, who love to repeat that "New York is not America," or that Boston, Philadelphia, the South and Washington are worlds apart. As a matter of fact, my superficial experience is that rarely does even the Middle Western bourgeois correspond to the imaginary pattern. They often hide strange thoughts and torments in their bald craniums and unconfessed passions under their double-breasted suits. But in the United States that is a secret which interests only psychiatrists, great poets, detectives and Doctor Kinsey.

The illusion has been preserved, also, because in the past Americans have had more frequent relations with those foreign people who easily confirmed their preconception, those whose superficial traits vaguely corresponded to the ideal pattern: the British, the Dutch, the Germans, the Scandinavians, for instance, whose differences from the mythical model could be ascribed to quaint local customs, Old World habits and folklore. Whenever the Americans were compelled by circumstances to recognize any fundamental difference between what they thought people should be and reality, they became irritated.

This irritation is worth deep study. It is usually interpreted abroad as the proof of their secret design to coerce all the inhabitants of the planet into "the American way of life," whether they like it or not, because their

"American way of life" seems to Americans vastly superior to anything else. This misunderstanding on the part of foreigners takes the form of anti-American criticism, ironical and bitter comment on gangsters, divorces, Hollywood movies, corruption, Coca-Cola and the comics. The interpretation, of course, is unjust. Americans are merely baffled when they discover that people are not what they were led to believe, that the cliché is false; they are as baffled as a motorist who recognizes suddenly that his road map is an imaginary one with little relation to the landscape around him. If a Calabrian farmer is contented with his oxcart and does not want a refrigerator, if the Corsican shepherd considers the height of *joie de vivre* killing his personal enemy and not driving a Cadillac, what can Americans do about these people, how can they help them, and, above all, who are they?

Thus their dealings with the unknown world, the Latins, the Levantines, the Orientals, the Slavs have always been very difficult. When a solitary American learned, after a lifetime study, the real character of such foreign people and could handle them well, he was no longer considered "a real American" by his compatriots and his advice was spurned. In *"partibus infidelium"* Americans tend to build a make-believe world around themselves, inhabited only by such local inhabitants who have learned, through personal inclination or design, to play the part expected of them of "nice" foreigners. They must love dogs and children, appreciate Christmas festivities, be apparently unable to lie, conduct intrigues or steal stamps; and they must be ready to admire machines and noble sentiments. Such people—the local staff of any American organization, public or private, the "*compradores*" in China, interpreters everywhere, hangers-on of American missions—while skillful at never deceiving their employers, are the worst possible liaison with their own countrymen. Their livelihood often depends on preserving their boss's illusions and isolation.

It was also true that no nation could surpass the United States in wealth and power. It had won all wars, against England twice, against Mexico, Spain, Pancho Villa, Central American bandits, Germany twice, Austria-Hungary, Turkey, and once even against its most difficult enemy, its own people. Taking too easily for granted that this obvious fact was accepted by all and that it was as plainly stated in other nations' schoolbooks as in their own, Americans have developed the habit of taking part in international disputes somewhat like Moses descending from Mount Sinai.

They always offered the tables of the law: the Monroe Doctrine, John Hay's Open Door notes, the Fourteen Points, the Kellogg Pact or the Atlantic Charter. They always considered it superfluous to see that adequate measures were taken for the enforcement of their desires. They apparently never suspected that the only covenants ever obeyed are those whose violation is more costly and dangerous than obedience. They thought that the mere expression of their point of view was sufficient, and they never really understood why practically nothing was ever done about their proposals or why the rest of the world paid them only a courteous, hypo-critical, and insincere attention. Did not foreign nations realize that the United States could, if willing, gather together the most powerful armies, the strongest navies, as it had done, late and with reluctance, several times in its history, when it had become absolutely necessary?

The British and the Romans had considered the inhab-itants of foreign parts barbarians and natives, not to be disturbed in their habits, incomprehensible and alien, to be controlled, administered, bettered, instructed, or repressed and coerced when necessary by all the means political experience had taught, alliances, prizes, threats, war or the installation of friendly chieftains. Nothing ever surprised the British and the Romans who con-sidered the most desperate and illogical behavior on the part of foreigners only natural. Everything is a surprise to Americans. Thus they constantly propose the theory that foreigners would much rather busy themselves with commerce, industry and the cultivation of their own gardens, but that, compelled by insane and cruel tyrants, they are sometimes involved in bloody adventures which are repugnant to their very nature. This is the reason why all American wars are made to liberate oppressed people and why they always ask for the severe punish-ment of the enemy leaders at the end.

All policy based principally on these two preconcep-tions, that people are fundamentally "human," i.e., cre-ated in the image of the American ideal, and that it is the worst taste to show one's muscles in public, is necessarily an abstract policy, designed for an ideal world, as it should be but is not yet. The American diplomatic representative in complicated circumstances tends to behave like the inexperienced suitor who looks at his love not as she is, with her low desires, weaknesses and defects, but as he imagines her, a divine and immaculate figure, with the result that others always end up in bed with her. This is a praiseworthy approach to a problem but scarcely fruitful. Franklin Roosevelt, for instance, saw Mao as an agrarian reformer and Harry Truman saw Joseph Stalin as "Uncle Joe."

The Marshall Plan, to which Europe owes reconstruction and salvation, and the world, peace, has deceived many Americans, who expected gratitude, good will and friendship as their reward, which they certainly would have gathered if they had spent the money between the States of Pennsylvania and Utah. All Europeans thought, and many wrote, that if the United States was willing to throw away so many billions of dollars, it certainly had its own private reasons, which foreigners could not see clearly, because nobody except the insane throws away money. This is not the case with the Americans. They believed that the United States was following a mysterious project of its own, in its own way, in defense of its own interests; and they concluded that no gratitude was due.

Such policies are a source of continuous misunderstanding, especially in the Middle East. An important American official in Washington, speaking of a minor Arab nation, sadly said to me, "We have given them a $20,000 dental clinic, and they don't like us." Mrs.

Grady, wife of a former American ambassador to Iran, thought of a good deed that needed to be done: Iranian children did not have a real playground as schoolboys have in the United States. She sent for all the apparatus from home, convinced the Shah to donate a plot of land, instructed local workmen how to set up the various swings and slides, and had a few trees planted around. One day the Court, the diplomatic corps, the government, and the local notables took part in an impressive inaugural ceremony. Mrs. Grady was congratulated for her initiative.

The first light of the following dawn illuminated Mrs. Grady's playground completely devastated, without slides, benches, swings, and the rest of the expensive equipment. Everything had been stolen during the night by people who knew the exact value of steel pipes, chains and wooden boards, in the Bazaar. (This is to be taken as a single case history and not a generalization. The present wife of the American ambassador in Iran has organized a medical dispensary, where she personally works long hours, and is very popular and loved by the local inhabitants.)

An American official in Tripoli was very worried, a couple of years ago, before the creation of the new kingdom. One day, he asked me, "Do you seriously think that, once they are an independent people, the Libyans will allow us to keep our Wheelus Field near Tripoli?" The directors of the Saudi Arabia Oil Company buy their peace every day by gifts and concessions to King

Ibn Saud and do not know how long they will be able to work unmolested at their oil drilling and pumping.

Middle Eastern problems are more instructive because they are simpler and less hypocritically couched in extraneous words than problems elsewhere. You usually see the wires. Politics there are based not on an abstract valuation of forces but on concrete, existing power— and on the will to use it. The powerful, in those countries, enrich and protect their friends, never accept slights or insults, and destroy their enemies without pity. If the powerful one does not behave according to this pattern, if he yields to pressure, it is the sign that, no matter what he may say to justify himself, no matter what humanitarian theories he may advocate, he is not really as strong as he wants people to believe, and therefore has no right to rule. It also means that it is dangerous to serve him, as he offers no protection to those who compromise themselves for him.

Of course, the powerful never clearly back their requests with an open threat or blackmail. Able and experienced men are they who never show force but are ready to use it at a moment's notice and who allow their opponents to yield honorably, saving their dignity. Powerful men also never take for granted that their adversaries are spotless gentlemen. They presume they are ready to defend their interests by any means, legitimate if possible, and illegitimate if necessary. Middle East people and Orientals have learned through the centuries that he who wants to win must be ready to lose without great sorrow and must be able to win without great joy, *sine spe sine metu*, with no hope nor fear, as the Romans knew. They always try to negotiate from a position of relative indifference, prepared for victory, defeat or a draw. There is nothing new about this and especially nothing that Americans have not known for centuries. It is the application to political transaction of the same knowledge of human nature which Americans use daily in their national card game, poker. It is therefore surprising to foreigners that the very same men who can beat them all hollow at the card table should be defenseless at the conference table, that the men who will not easily believe you hold four aces will accept at face value your own declaration of disinterested and progressive motives without calling your bluff.

A veteran French diplomat stationed in Washington, an acute observer of the American scene, said to me a few months ago, "I wonder why they don't send somebody like Frank Costello as ambassador-at-large to the Middle East. He would know how to handle men and problems." Of course, the Frenchman admitted, Costello himself would not be the best man, for his name had been too openly associated with rackets. But an upright and honorable person would be useful who had made a study of Costello's venerable technique, the art of using power to enrich friends and to destroy enemies, the art of the threat which does not have to be spoken, for all people prefer being an ally rather than an opponent. The Costello manner is too gross, too obvious and too cynical. He has used his technique merely for the advancement of evil. Why should it be difficult to use it in the advancement of good? What prevents Americans from recognizing the fundamental identity of human affairs? Why must they always confuse the ship and her cargo, the art of navigation and the port of destination?

It may be that the very beliefs and habits which have comforted Americans in their work and which have helped them build within a few generations the greatest power the world has seen out of a wild and unexplored continent, prevent them now from seeing clearly and coherently in international affairs and from assuming fully and wisely their new burdens. If the forefathers' ideals were right and if they were the highest achievement of human thought (that they were right has been proved by their success), it was only natural for Americans to think that anybody ignoring them, refusing them or opposing them was on the wrong track. It also followed that anybody who wanted to adopt them should be encouraged and helped. That those ideals were only partly responsible for the Americans' success is a theory which only skeptical scholars have explored. For most Americans, what was good enough for Thomas Jefferson and Benjamin Franklin is still good enough for them.

Take war, for instance. Love of peace was among the foundations of the American system. Wars were notoriously made by foreigners out of their mad desire for blood, riches, and power. One could usually make war or not, according to one's desires, Americans believed, and all that one had to do was to turn one's back to the world and look after one's own business. The frontier with Canada was always pointed to with great pride: so many miles of unguarded border and never a shot fired. If things came to the worst, they could always rely on two things, the Atlantic Ocean and their ancient capacity to face emergencies. Wars for them have always been, on a national scale, what was, on a smaller scale, the village fire. The bells tolled, everybody rushed to the scene, worked day and night, the men carrying pails, pumping water, or tearing down walls, the women preparing coffee and sandwiches, taking care of the children and the injured, all this without rest, until the flames were extinguished. Then they all went back to bed. The system worked well enough from 1776 till the last war.

How can Americans now quickly adapt themselves to the permanent war, which has to be prepared, threatened, feared or fought, cold or hot, every day of their future national life? How can they be shown that the peace they enjoyed was not the just reward of their prudence but the fruit of other people's—mostly those of the British—past wars and readiness to make future wars? Americans naturally tend to rely on their old experiences. The temptation is always with them to rush into whatever there is to be done, do it, and get it over with. Who will tell them the flames will never be extinguished and they will never go back to bed?

Or take their political ideals. What is wrong with them

and what is wrong with encouraging foreigners who
want to adopt them? The Chinese crisis, for instance,
started about fifty years ago, when democratic ideals
carelessly left around, mostly by American missionaries
and teachers, helped bring about the collapse of the old
decayed Empire. The destruction of any order is easy
work, like blasting a building with dynamite. But construction is a difficult job. Nations must create their own
new structures out of their own suffering, experience,
past and their ideas. They can never borrow other people's constitutions, except as a façade which usually hides
a shameful reality. Over the ruins of the old order, anarchy always prevails. After anarchy, dictatorship. Dic-
tators are unpleasant, sometimes inspired by Marxist
doctrines, always opposed to democracy. Some believe
that Mao's victory was partly prepared by the money
which the Chinese Empire paid to the United States
after the Boxer Rebellion and the United States dedicated to scholarships for Chinese students in American
universities. Dwight Eisenhower, in his inaugural address,
reminded his countrymen of this danger: "We shall never
use our strength to try to impress upon another people
our own cherished political and economic institutions."
Still, one seldom has to use one's strength: American
diplomatic representatives can scarcely keep themselves
from encouraging weakly but effectively any revolution
that looks to them like their own old one. The British
suspect the Iranians' decision to nationalize oil had been
encouraged by the American ambassador in Teheran,
who thought at first the Iranians were to be congratu-

lated. Naguib had more than one pat on the back from Mr. Caffery. North Africa is in turmoil over the Americans' anti-colonial attitude. Illiterate Arabs expect the United States to take the place of France as the dominating power (because the simple natives can only understand a struggle between competing ambitions), and they look forward to the day when the flags over the barracks will change and the rich, easygoing, sentimental Americans will be left alone with them.

When he was High Commissioner in Germany, I asked John J. McCloy one question: "You have spent a lot of money and you have given great care to the education of the German people in the democratic way of life. How did the experiment go, in your opinion?" He answered by telling me two stories.

The first: A group of American officers had been invited by a Hessian Count to his shooting preserves for a day's sport. He was provided with a gun for the day, in spite of strict prohibitions. During the morning the Count saw somebody move through the bushes, a man wearing an old, discarded military uniform, as vagrants do in Germany, who walked stealthily and suspiciously. In loud German words, the Count ordered him to stop three times, then raised his gun and killed him. He turned out to be one of his guests, an American officer wearing old clothes for the day, who was trying to approach the game without being seen. The Count was immediately arrested and charged with murder. His defense was based on two main points: "I didn't know he was an officer," and "I didn't know he was an American."

He apparently believed that he would have been fully justified in killing a German, of any rank, but had made a mistake when he had killed an American, and one belonging to the officer class. McCloy received hundreds of letters from the inhabitants of the Count's village, asking for his release. They were all inspired by the same sentiments. How could the local squire be jailed? What would become of his people? they asked.

The second story: Every time the High Commissioner was considering the fate of war criminals in United States Occupation Forces jails, thousands of letters reached his desk, asking for the release of this or that man. A study of these pleas showed that the great majority were written by humble people in defense of Field Marshals, generals, and high-ranking officials; most of the writers were shocked by the idea that such exalted personages should be shut up in common jails with criminals. Practically nobody wrote in defense of the soldiers and petty officers, who really could be considered less guilty as most of them had obeyed superior orders.

Mr. McCloy said, "Naturally, American ideas have had some effect. Sometimes I suspect we have mostly convinced our friends and left our enemies untouched. People who had a natural bent for our way of doing things were eager to learn. The others admired a few American traits, our efficiency, our machines, our financial capacity, perhaps, and seldom bothered to go to the source of our power, which is liberty. Some Germans follow our leadership only because we have defeated them. Has our experiment been successful? I wish I could say yes. I don't know. It will take years to know. It will depend on how history will develop in the next few decades, whether our kind of Germans will be able to keep the leadership of their country and whether the rest of the world will find it convenient to go on admiring our ideals."

On the other hand, Americans cannot help being themselves. The Chinese empire looked rotten to them and not to them alone; they said so and did what they could about it, raising a new Chinese intelligentsia in American universities, spending millions of dollars for missions, libraries, institutes of learning and hospitals. Colonial domination appears to them the unfair, inefficient, and barbarous system it is; and they have been against it since 1776, even when the dominating power was their own country. They did not fight and win two wars against the Germans to allow them to go on believing the same old myths. Germans notoriously tend to go back to uniforms as soon as other people's backs are turned and to start new wars as soon as they can afford it. Why not try to show them the utter waste of their philosophy of life? At the back of the Americans' desire to straighten out the ills of the world, to spread to other people the benefits of their spiritual way of life, is not only, as many think, a provincial feeling of superiority, but also the humble desire to see other people share the benefits which Americans enjoy and which they consider the birthright of any human being, and the hope to see things settled once and for all. This, too, must be considered, that the United States is not an isolated planet, that her ideas have ancient European origins, that the Americans' way of life is really the Western man's inevitable future and not their own invention, and that there is little Americans can do to prevent other people from imitating them and following their example. Their mere existence, living as they do, would have influenced the world, the Chinese empire, colonial people, or democratic Germans, whether the State Department wanted to or not. This is not always their fault and not always a bad thing.

Unable to be anything but Americans, it is not surprising that they should have given such magic importance to raising everybody's standard of living. Hungry people are easy prey to revolution, of course. Nobody likes to die of starvation. Famine and unemployment are notoriously the worst political advisers. Well-fed people, on the other hand, seldom compare their prosperous condition to the suffering they have avoided and do not think of it as a point of arrival, not even in the United States, and instead of praising the Lord and enjoying their food, embitter their lives in the attempt always to find new causes of discontent. The Founding Fathers knew this when they wrote "the pursuit" and not the "achievement of happiness." The billions spent to help Europe and the rest of the world, the Marshall Plan and Point Four, are to be considered like international health projects, plague or yellow fever control measures, which try to prevent the spreading of disease but scarcely justify the hope that men will spend their lives thinking of the horrible death they avoided and the epidemics which could have swept their country but did not.

Communism is only partly caused by poverty. It is not a medieval protest of the disinherited, like the Lollards, but is mostly the illusion of an easy answer to the problems of people who have been torn from an old way of life and have not found peace in the new. American officials in Italy found proof of this when they discovered that party membership was highest in the more advanced and richer provinces, in the industrial North and in the prosperous farming regions in Romagna, Emilia, and Tuscany, lowest in the South, where people were living on the margin between starvation and death. It was also discovered that wherever, at the Americans' prompting, agrarian reform was carried out and large land holdings were parceled out among the poor peasantry, as in Calabria, the number of local communists swelled. The new members were mostly the people who had either received a new farm from the government and were not satisfied or had not received one and were disappointed.

An Italian Liberal *deputato* recently said to me, "Take the owner of a flock of sheep. He works twenty or more hours a day, sleeps on the ground, eats stale bread and is contented. He watches his own sheep grow by the hour. Every kilo gained, every wisp of wool, is lire in his pocket. Nobody can ask a hired man to keep similar hours. That is the heart of the matter. Why is it that we can't make working for others with good wages, short hours, and all kinds of benefits in a modern industrial organization, as satisfactory as watching one's own sheep? Money is only a partial answer."

Evidently, no money at all would make matters worse. No Marshall Plan, no Point Four, no "offshore purchases" would have allowed the epidemic of communism to spread and destroy the peace of the world. It is better to parcel out large, unused landholdings among small farmers than to leave the land idle and the population starving. It is better to spread new industrial techniques, to encourage production, to create jobs for men, than to leave things as they are. There is nothing wrong with all these American initiatives. What *is* wrong is the Americans' hopes of immediate results.

Mr. Truman recalled the workings of his mind—a good example of the American mind—on June 25, 1950, when the North Koreans attacked. "I was in Independence, Missouri," he said, "when Secretary Acheson telephoned me and gave me the news. Flying back over the flatlands of the Middle West and over the Appalachians, that summer afternoon, I had a lot of time to think. I turned the problem over in my mind in many ways, but my thoughts kept coming back to the nineteen thirties, to Manchuria, Ethiopia, the Rhineland, Austria, and finally to Munich. Here was history repeating itself. Here was another probing action, another testing action. If we let the Republic of Korea go under some other country would be next and then another. And all the time the courage and confidence of the free world would be ebbing away, just as it did in the nineteen thirties. And the United Nations would go the way of the League of Nations."

As the late Otto Kahn had told me many years ago, Americans never try to foresee in their imagination the probable course of events, the consequences of any decisions; they must always experiment and make mistakes. They must live through the nineteen thirties, see the League of Nations go under, do nothing about Manchuria, the Rhineland, Ethiopia, and Austria; and *then* they know, they have learned, they will try not to make the same mistake all over again. It is an expensive way, but their only way.

What is wrong is not the American ideals but the excessive hopes with which Americans accompany all decisions. Most of their moves are good but vitiated by the mirage of immediate revolutionary accomplishments. The world is always being transformed from its foundations. Palingenesis is just around the corner. The clash with reality later turns their unreasonable hopes inevitably to impatience, then to disappointment, and finally to cynicism. The course can be followed in any of the many problems Americans tried to solve after the war. Europe, for instance: the unreasonable hopes of the

Marshall Plan, which would unite Europe, strengthen her, rearm her against the common enemy, all within five years; then the impatience with Europeans, who did not realize the urgency of the situation, the disappointment with France, Britain, Germany, all trying to serve their national interests in spite of the Americans' suggestions; and finally cynicism, the tired sensation that all the money was being thrown down the waste pipe, "Operation Rat Hole" it was called.

Or Russia: the unreasonable hopes that the late Joseph Vissarionovich Dzhugashvili, in spite of his police record, was really a Rotarian in disguise; the impatience with the Russians' misunderstanding of the United States' intentions; the resigned and hopeless cynicism of today.

Or take Korea: the unreasonable hope that nothing would happen, even if the United States occupation forces were reduced to just enough soldiers to mount guard at the United States ambassador's office; the impatience and indignation when the attack came; and finally the cynical and resigned acceptance of a never-ending, costly, and apparently meaningless war.

At the bottom of these excessive hopes there may be apathy. Men who get out of bed only for the greatest crusades—to change the face of the world, and to right all wrongs for ever—are apparently reluctant to accept everyday nonrevolutionary tasks. Or again, there may be fear. Why are Americans always looking frenziedly for a magic wand, a new machine, a gadget, a political formula, one word ("containment" or "liberation"), if not to be rid of their anxiety? The atom bomb has been surrounded by the attributes of an all-destroying and all-beneficent god. The statute of the United Nations was welcomed by some of the United States' best brains not as a gentle, Utopian experiment, but as a foolproof recipe for peace, the dawn of a new era of brotherhood.

Little word-machines fascinate Americans: Maginot Lines of legal paragraphs, pacts, covenants, resolutions, agreements, statements, pronouncements, to which they openly attribute almost supernatural powers, while privately they know, and show it in their everyday behavior, that a contract is only as good as the power behind it, that a pact will be considered holy only as long as it will be to the advantage of the various parties to keep it and that social or international peace is not the product of words and sentiments but, like the equilibrium of heavenly bodies, the product of contrasted and balanced forces.

Then again, they may need fear. How could Congress pass the armed forces budget and foreign aid appropriations, taxpayers pay their huge income taxes, soldiers go to the front and face death, women go without luxuries, statesmen invent new daring policies, unless a terrible and obvious danger was imminent? The press is full of terrifying stories of Soviet war preparations, their aggressive intentions, the evil minds of the Kremlin schemers, the subtle infiltration of communists into the most delicate sectors of federal bureaucracy. Large maps always show fat red arrows sweeping unopposed across Europe from the Russian border. Russian bombers, carrying H-bombs, always cross the United States borders unharmed and undetected to pulverize every major American city. Most of these stories are true. The danger is real. What is wrong is only the emphasis, the urgency, the timidity behind them. The popularity of Senator McCarthy is probably a proof of this need to fear. Another proof is the eagerness with which the public welcomes the weakest Russian peace gestures.

Fear, real or imaginary, muddles all thinking and makes relations with enemies and allies extremely difficult. Americans have acquired the habit of talking out loud to reassure themselves. Politicians and military men openly debate problems with the self-confidence of a man telling his wife, in the secret of their bedroom, what he plans to say the next day to his boss. Naturally, no man ever told the boss the exact words he announced to his wife, and no American Secretary of State has fortunately told European Foreign Ministers the blunt warning and threatening words which he had used to the American public over television a few days before. No responsible military man, in command of divisions in the field, can accomplish the daring maneuvers which he himself will describe, when retired on his pension, to newspapermen.

Fear, real or imaginary, makes all officials boast of their plans and decisions so often that enemies can always prepare for a new threat. Fear makes American negotiators almost as bad as Russians, who are always afraid they will not be alive the next day to read what *Pravda* will say. Allies know how anxious Americans are not to be left alone, and they sell their moral help at the highest price. All they have to do is to hand back to the American ambassador the first State Department note as "unacceptable" and wait, as one walks out of the antique shop saying "the price is too high" when one wants to get a reduction. Enemies who read the American papers are clearly told how much Americans hope to reach an agreement, a *modus vivendi*, a truce, and always try to make the best of their knowledge.

Here again, international behavior is mysteriously in contrast with the Americans' private virtues. They have never been easily scared. It may be, as we have said, that the diligent cultivation of fear is indispensable to a people who can only be great under stress, who need a fire-breathing dragon to slay first in order to get a girl; but it is an insecure and wasteful foundation on which to construct a lasting edifice. There has been no example in history of an empire built on fear. Fear has merely preserved tottering organizations for short spells, before their final collapse. Is this fear real, and is it really necessary?

One evening, last winter, I was coming back to the mainland from the Dutch island of Overflakkee, flooded by the sea. I had been with a British "Ducks" detachment looking for corpses. The ferry carried a stack of full coffins on the top deck (they had been empty that morning), shivering refugees in the salon, tired soldiers and journalists. I sat below deck, drinking coffee and talking with a Dutch colleague, when, just before the boat sailed, an American Air Force major got on. He was visibly exhausted. The American occupation forces in Germany had sent men, planes, food, medical supplies almost before the storm had ceased. Americans were busy everywhere dropping supplies and rubber boats from planes, picking survivors off trees and roofs by helicopters. The American probably had not taken off his clothes for days.

The Dutch journalist looked at him, then touched my elbow, and said, *"Luftwaffe."* He was no communist, just a quiet, diligent, democratic Dutch reporter, devoted to the Royal House. I asked, "What did you say?" He repeated, *"Luftwaffe.* We know them. We have seen them before." The tired major sat down in an empty seat, pulled his cap over his eyes, and dozed off. He was very far from home.

Disconcerting comments of this kind can be picked up everywhere in Europe, not only among communists or fascists, who are professional United States haters, but among moderate middle-class, timid people. Often one hears this in Paris: "Thank God for the men in the Politburo. They are the ones who really save the peace." Naturally, it is meant as a joke. But the chuckles and the looks that always go with the words show that people believe there is some truth in them, that Americans are really too hot-headed and hysterical to be entrusted with the destinies of the world, but that fortunately the Russians are cautious and realistic men. The last to tell me a variation of the theme was a French cabinet minister who, after Stalin's death, said, "This man Malenkov is a fat bureaucrat. Fat bureaucrats don't go to war. War disarranges their files and routines. Thank God we have him there." A good joke, again, like calling the United States Air Force the *Luftwaffe*.

Still, when one sees so many people everywhere, in Athens, Rome, Milan, Paris, Brussels, smile when they talk about the United States, chuckle at the latest American declaration of policy, find joy in the failure of the latest American project or wonder-working machine ("Their jets are not nearly half as good as the Russians' and the motors are British anyway"), and retell the latest bright saying of a United States diplomat or traveler ("A lady from Texas said in Cairo the other day to a very high Egyptian official: 'Back home they think you're colored, but *we* know better'") one concludes that something is wrong somewhere. When you press the point, when you ask for a serious opinion, all irony vanishes and you usually get a sober answer.

"Nobody in Europe doubts that the leadership of the free world rests with the United States," said a British official to me recently. "We know that if the Americans had withdrawn from international affairs we would have been lost." On the other hand an Italian columnist said, "Naturally, we know they believe the things we do, they are defending our civilization which is also theirs. Still, sometimes we can't help being more afraid of them than of the Russians."

Very little of this appears in the moderate press (except in *Le Monde*, the French neutralist paper). Nothing is ever said directly to the Americans, across the green baize tables, at the many international conferences. No politician is willing to be quoted directly on anything resembling a criticism of the United States. Still, the atmosphere is poisoned by unspoken thoughts, relations are complicated by mists of empty words, State Department pet projects bog down amidst the insincere applause of everybody concerned and the solemn promises that something certainly will be done in the near future.

Americans are often irritated by all this. A high Washington official said this to Raymond Aron, a French political writer, who quoted him in *Le Figaro:* "Why do your politicians feel compelled to come to Washington to express to us the high sentiments which they themselves deny in their private conversations? Do they think we are bigger fools than we are? We would like less official sentiments and more concordance between words and action, between the decisions of ministers and their drawing-room quips. We do not dislike those who tell us frankly where they stand. We dislike those who say Yes to our faces and No behind our backs."

Apparently all Europeans feel that it is unsafe to explain matters as they see them to the Americans, that it is better to humor them, to keep them happy, as they would not understand why foreigners often adopt a cautious attitude about problems which look extremely simple to the State Department, which have been studied by experts, and on which all relevant data have been gathered and classified. The attitude is a human one, part of the traditional courtesy and *savoir-vivre* of the older continent. One does not contradict the boss, even when he gets odd and ruinous ideas in his head. One merely smiles, approves and does what one can to offset the impending catastrophe.

Something is wrong, somewhere. Nobody knows exactly what it is. A collection of European criticisms of the United States, gathered from London to Istanbul, cannot be arranged according to a coherent pattern. Several recurring themes, however, can be identified. The principal one is the inevitable irritation and embarrassment felt by once proud nations who are now reduced to beg for their living, survival and safety. They are not on a regular allowance. They must literally fill forms with their requirements, year after year. They are forbidden to earn what they need with exports to the American market; they are prevented from trading with the Marxist world; they are strictly kept in a precarious condition; and they must wait the pleasure of Congress before they know how much money they will be allowed to have.

They all agree that uncertain aid is better than none. On the other hand, they all are bluntly forced to recognize the fact that they can have no policy of their own, that no decision they make has any value and that all matters are decided at the Capitol. This resentment is felt more sharply among the winning allies of the last war, the British and the French, than in Germany and Italy, where people consider their diminished status the inev-

itable outcome of defeat. It is easier to accept graceless
alms from one's conqueror than from one's old friend.

The reaction would probably be inevitable, no matter
what the American government did about aid to Europe,
as nobody likes a benefactor, everybody hates the boss,
discipline, restraint, other people's thoughts and ways of
doing things. It cannot be denied, at the same time, that
very little is done in the United States to allow Europeans to forget their weakness and their dependent status. Once in a while an American politician will utter a
few empty words as devoid of significance as the European ministers' expressions of noble sentiments, to explain that aid is "mutual," that we are all on the same
footing, the big and the small. Little is done to change
the paternalistic attitude or to give back to Europe some
of her old independence. The arrangement is an unhealthy and precarious one which makes nobody happy.
Americans complain because it costs them too much
money, the Europeans because they are humiliated by
the gifts and by the manner with which they are given.
Some even suspect that behind it there may be a vast
project to save the American economy from collapse, at
the expense of European foreign trade, self-respect, and
prosperity.

On this point, communist and many democratic econ-
omists agree. They point out that American agricultural
production has been overdeveloped, that the government is forced to purchase surplus products to defend
the purchasing power of the farmers, that the collapse of

farm prices is always the first sign of an economic crisis in the United States, that one of the ways to finance farmers is to pay foreigners to consume their products and that as soon as foreigners cannot buy American farm products prices slump and the malaise spreads slowly to all sectors.

The second most important cause of misunderstanding seems to be the incapacity of most Europeans to understand the functioning of the United States. The Washington dispatches they read in their morning papers usually scare them to death. The American scene seems populated by raving maniacs. The maniacs usually get the bigger headlines, both in Europe and in the United States. The sane seldom say such interesting and provocative things. Generals propose dropping atomic bombs almost everywhere, or come up with patented plans to win this, that, or the other war, hot or cold, money back if not satisfied. Correspondents reveal that nobody in Washington has the vaguest idea of what to do about this or that urgent and dangerous problem, and that there is no machinery to work out a solution. One authority says that the United States is ready for all events, that it will destroy any aggressor within a matter of minutes. Another great authority declares, at about the same time, that all American cities can be pulverized without warning. One learns that the American armed forces are the strongest and most modern anywhere and that their equipment, training, clothing, supply organization, planning and morale are complicated, obsolete, shabby, impractical and unrealistic. One learns that there was never enough ammunition in Korea, that United States forces shot more than twice the number of rounds they used in Europe during World War II, that they shot ten times more than the enemy, that they had ammunition to spare. One reads that corrupt politicians or experts have squandered billions in useless projects, that high-ranking State Department officials forget secret documents at cocktail parties and that senators are about to cut all aid to foreign countries and the armed forces budget, too.

It would be easy to point an accusing finger at European correspondents from Washington (it has often been done) and charge them with poisoning the international atmosphere. Most of these confusing dispatches, however, originate from the American news agencies themselves, who gather the facts, write the stories, polish, edit, and transmit them to all the world over one of the most modern and rapid systems of communication the world has seen. Some of these stories are even broadcast by the Voice of America, with apparent complacency, probably to show that freedom is not afraid of contradictions.

All this paralyzes foreigners with apprehension. Some suspect that Americans do not really know what they are doing or where they are going. Every problem seems to be worked out in a vacuum, completely isolated from other problems and cut away from historic precedents. Take European rearmament, for instance. The United States asks Western Europe to rearm urgently, to spend sums much beyond her possibilities, because a grave threat menaces the peace, and the enemy can cross the border at any minute. Preparations to rearm will last several years. Will this terrible aggressive enemy wait until Europe is rearmed and ready to defend herself? And if the enemy does, does that not mean that he is not as aggressive as the Americans paint him? The United States then believes in supernational organizations, one is also frequently told. There are at present several supernational organizations, the French Union, for instance, and the British Commonwealth, which the State Department sometimes seems to do what it can to discourage and divide into their components.

Edouard Bonnefous, a French Député, spoke of this a while ago: "Is it logical that while promoting the supernational ideal and asking nations like ours to accept major cuts in their sovereignty, they should at the same time work in an absolutely contrary direction, trying to awaken sovereignties which never existed and which rest on no real basis?"

The United States, one learns, spent billions to encourage the free exchange of goods. Then, one learns further, it does what it can to discourage the importation of those very goods for whose production Europeans are better equipped, trained and endowed, the goods they produce at lower costs than the American competitors, like watches, or those that cannot be reproduced in the United States, like Gorgonzola cheese, thus contradicting the eighteenth-century canons immortalized by Adam Smith, one of the moral founders of the republic. Or take freedom and human dignity for which we must

all fight. Monsieur Jules Moch, very often a cabinet minister in France, a Socialist, told this little story in the
Chambre des Députés, a short time ago, "I was going to
New York on one of the French liners when the new
McCarran Act was first applied. An American government inspector got on board at Le Havre. I happened to
tell him that it was not one of the French habits to ask a
chambermaid, for instance, whether she habitually prac-
ticed prostitution. I must say that the question got him
the following answer from the woman, followed by a
weeping fit: 'If I were one of those I would not be working as a chambermaid on a liner at fifty-two years of
age.'"

What knowledge of human nature and of human affairs drives inspectors to ask, in the name of the United
States government, whether fifty-two-year-old cham-
bermaids, of all people, are addicted to loose and mer-
cenary love habits? Is this the respect for the divine dignity of man for the defense of which we are allied and
ready to fight?

Now nations dominated by the Soviet must be won
over to the West by means of intensified psychological
persuasion and then liberated with all available means
except actual warfare. A bulletin of the West German
Social Democratic Party recently commented, "There is
no known case in the history of dictatorships when psychological warfare from the outside has led to the fall
of a tyranny or has even seriously endangered it. National socialism and fascism fell under the impact of
attacks from outside and the Spanish dictatorship con-

tinues to exist to this day. In any case the Soviets have over a period of more than a generation made secure their hold on the Russian people, even if with the most brutal means. Is it the intention to effect the insurrection of a people who have only limited access to radios by way of the Voice of America? That would appear to be an infantile conception."

European governments are rapped on their knuckles because they do not do their homework, do not prepare detailed rearmament plans, or because they have not brought their divisions to scheduled levels at the right time. On the other hand, no Western European Minister of Defense is able to know a year before how much aid he is going to get from the United States and whether he can count on such aid in the future. Promised shipments of arms, tanks, supplies, and matériel seldom arrive on time, and sometimes divisions are formed and trained months before their equipment lands.

Then again we are told emphatically and earnestly that we must defend "Spiritual Values," the only ones worth preserving, against the onslaught of "Godless Materialism"; and we all agree. To prove the point we are always shown propaganda pictures of the American way of life which can hardly be described as the triumph of the spirit: huge new chromium-plated cars, electronic washing machines, deep freezers which could hide a whole ox, luxurious homes, splendid clothes, overfed and smiling workers, cows, pigs, children, and fat dignitaries of all kinds. We are told that some of the United States Cabinet members are worthy and virtuous gentlemen who were able to amass large private fortunes; people in Western Europe know that those among them who amass large private fortunes may be considered able, active, astute, ruthless, but not necessarily disinterested or honorable.

Starving Sicilians, who would like nothing better than to abandon their sun-baked, parched island in order to emigrate to the United States, where they can join their relatives and countrymen, are shown at great expense documentaries depicting the abundant life of the country where they are forbidden to go by the Immigration Act, gigantic projects to dam big rivers and irrigate arid lands to make them blossom and produce fabulous wealth. All of us are shown the biggest granaries, factories, stadiums, hospitals, bridges, parking lots, skyscrapers in the world; undoubtedly signs of success, industry, perseverance, thrift, but scarcely proof of the American love for Spiritual Values per se.

Western Europeans do not know the United States. They think it is a country like their own, to be judged according to the same principles. They do not know the great American contradictions, the fatal choice between a noble crusade or utter indifference, the eternal struggle toward completing the forefathers' dream, the refusal to accept the world as it has always been, history as the ancients had known it, human nature as Christ himself recognized it. In comparison with the United States, where apparently anything can happen at any moment, Russia sometimes looks like a familiar monster, a huge, heartless bureaucratic tyranny, which usually behaves according to its own rules, whose moves can be reasonably predicted.

Giuseppe Pella, Italian Minister of the Budget, a redhaired economist from Piemonte, who is responsible for checking inflation in Italy and for having made the lira one of the hardest of the soft currencies, was traveling a few months ago between New York and Washington. He was sitting in the dining car with his secretaries, aides, and experts. They were going to debate some grave problems with Department of State experts. There were six Italians. Three sat with the Minister, two more at a nearby table. A large American businessman took one of the empty seats and courteously asked who all those foreigners were. One of them answered, "We are an Italian financial mission on its way to Washington. The man over there is the Italian Minister of the Budget." The American businessman turned to Giuseppe Pella and asked in a loud voice, "And how many millions are you going to ask for, this time, Mr. Minister?"

That not even Americans are happy about their foreign policy was shown by the last elections. The campaign also proved that few people knew what was wrong with it. Some critics asked for more of the same but with added zest, some for less of the same, some for a return to the happy days of Calvin Coolidge, and some, for the sake of preserving peace, for such violent measures as could easily provoke the largest and most devastating war the world has ever seen.

I tried to conduct my private survey before the elections.

Friday night, at Detroit. Businessmen abandon all thoughts of work, duty, and family, to gather at the Detroit Athletic Club, for stag cocktails and dinners. Lesser people stop at the entresol, in the public rooms. Greater men go upstairs to private apartments, leased by little satellite clubs, where they do not have to defend their dignity and protect themselves from importunate members who propose business deals. An English friend and I were the guests of one called the "Friday Night Study Club." The rooms looked like a regimental officers' mess. On the walls were stuffed animals' heads, varnished fishes, caricatures of friends, girls' pictures, photographs, with jocular dedications of deceased members. Negro servants in blue tailcoats with gold buttons passed the drinks. The friends (old businessmen, baldheaded, the pallor of the board rooms on their faces, shining new teeth in the flaccid cheeks) were still saddened by the memory of their offices, and their everyday personalities. They talked seriously of stock quotations, the international situation, steel production, prices. They may also have been embarrassed by the presence of the two strange foreigners.

Then, as the evening proceeded and more glasses were emptied, they became gradually gayer and more frivolous. They started clapping each other's shoulders, calling each other by ribald nicknames, recalling past anecdotes, and gently insulting each other, as embarrassed boys would. Dinner was served in a larger room, in front of a large painting of a naked woman lying on a fur-covered couch, wearing a large velvet hat and black silk stockings. The servants helped the men, who were a little unsteady by now, to sit down. In the growing confusion the waiters quietly got the orders and served dinner. Some members were getting up to telephone long distance to some forgotten school friend whose name had suddenly come to their mind, some were telling jokes in a loud voice which they never could finish, as they burst out laughing before the end, some were getting up to whisper mysterious words in a friend's ear, and the neighbor on my right was saying that he was not born to work in an office, that he cared little for money, that he had had other ideals in his youth which he had betrayed.

After dinner, after watching a fight on television, one of our guests, the publisher of an important Detroit daily, started talking. He was sunk in a large armchair, with an empty glass in his hand, a strange expression on his face, his eyes shining with emotion and indignation. When he started speaking, a sudden frightened silence fell on everybody. They all tried to stop him, saying, "Bob, you don't know what you're talking about," "This is not in the spirit of the evening," and "You forget your duties as a host." He went stubbornly on. He said, "Now that we have you two here I think it is only fitting that somebody tell you exactly what we, in America, think. You're costing us too much money."

The others whispered in our ears, "Don't pay any attention. He's drunk. He is an odd fellow. He doesn't mean what he says."

He went on, "We are tired of supporting you. We've wasted billions of dollars on Europe and what did we get in return? You are always in the same place. No progress. The British want to live like gentlemen on our dough. The Italians maintain the biggest Communist Party outside Russia. What do you do to defend yourselves? Here we pay terrific taxes, we accept a life of sacrifice, we work ourselves to the bone, the men at the conveyor belts and we in the damned offices, five days a week. We can't do everybody's work, pay for everybody, and fight for the whole world. If Europe is tired, discouraged, and cowardly, why, let her go her own way to ruin. I believe we are ruining you if we allow you to think that we are ready to go on working for you forever. I feel great decisions will have to be taken. American policy will have to change. Somebody has to tell you. I've told you."

The others protested, and when my friend and I answered the publisher's little speech they applauded heartily. Still we felt that when no foreigners were present, everybody thought more or less like Bob. They only thought it was not the hospitable thing to do, to tell us the truth after a good dinner.

Colonel Robert R. McCormick's office is on the twenty-fourth floor of the Tribune Tower in Chicago. His secretary, a little affable old woman, asked me to sit near her in the outer office, because I was to wait a few minutes. The colonel had arrived that very morning from Washington in his own plane. He had all the editors in his room for a *tour d'horizon*. The fact that the secretary was the only old secretary I had ever seen in the United States puzzled me, and I asked her about it. She told me that the colonel was very careful and conservative, that he wanted nobody around whom he had not known for a long time, which made it difficult to find successors when anybody died, and also restricted the number of people he saw, because he always wanted to know exactly who they were. She also asked me how I had got an appointment. I said it was my secret. Finally, with a slow metallic buzzing, a door swung mechanically open. Men came out in single file, each clutching to his chest a pad and pencil, each nodding in agreement to the last words a booming voice from the hidden room was sending after them.

The colonel was standing behind his desk when I was ushered in. The room was paneled with walnut, in the style of a French château drawing room and feebly illuminated by small lights, like a chapel. The door closed behind me, electrically, with the slow and fatal move-

ment of a bank safe closing for the night and disappeared
in the wainscoting as it had been artfully cut within the
frame of one of the panels. There was no handle to it.
Colonel McCormick is extremely tall—gigantic by Mediterranean standards—and everything in the room was
cut to his size. The marble-covered table came up to my
chest, the wastepaper baskets to my hips, the leather
armchairs were large enough for two men.

We sat on a couch. In the dim light the colonel looked
very pale, tired, worried, almost haggard. He watched
me carefully and said, "So you're Italian. My thoughts
are simple. I have no doubt, no matter what other people say, that the defense of Western Europe, within limits, and the struggle against communistic imperialism are
the necessary foundations of our foreign policy. Nevertheless, I ask myself if the sums spent in the past have
been properly and wisely invested to get the best results.
You see, it is a complicated matter. How much security
can we buy with one million dollars? How should we
spend it to get the maximum? That's where I disagreed
with the Democratic administration. Mass aid like that
we gave England and France [he did not mention Italy,
of course] are medicines which weaken the patient and
retard his recovery, for he needs more and more drugs
and cannot go without them."

To let me out the colonel kicked a little brass plate,
a little higher than the floor, on the right of the invisible
door, and the panel started opening slowly with the
usual mechanical buzzing. I wondered what would happen if Colonel McCormick fell sick one day, too weak to

kick the brass plate himself. On the corridor outside his rooms, as in all corridors of the building, were red arrows pointing in one direction and signs saying "Atomic Shelter."

"Our mistakes," said Senator Wiley of Wisconsin, sipping the famous bean soup in the Senate restaurant, "and we make many, are due in great part to our impatience. We always want to see within a few years revolutionary results which take generations to come about. I am in favor of our foreign policy. We aim well. I'm opposed to excessive optimism. You see, we're good-hearted people, we're good people, accustomed to miracles in our own country, and we can't bear to see others suffer. Did you see what has become of California in the last ten years? You should see our Northwest. You can't do the same abroad, apparently. We always want to do too much for too many people and too quickly."

One day in New York, I went to see Mr. Herbert Hoover, who is the representative of a strain of the American type so pure that he could be a character out of several old-fashioned American novels. He is a Quaker, the descendant of an old family (Andreas

Huber, German-born son of Swiss parents, came to America from Ellerstadt, in the Palatinate, in 1738), which had reached Iowa in four jumps and four generations. Orphaned, he was brought up by an uncle, a Federal Indian Agent, and played with the little Osage boys who taught him to shoot arrows and read the signs in the forest, like a trapper in Fenimore Cooper's books.

"The Friends," he says in his memoirs, "always held strongly to education, thrift, and individual enterprise. In consequence of plain living and hard work, poverty has never been their lot. So far as I know no member has ever been in jail or on public relief." The two things, jail and relief, are for him almost on the same plane. He made his way in the world, graduated from Stanford University, showed uncommon business sense in managing the football team, worked as a miner in a Nevada gold mine, was hired by an Australian mining company as an expert, was shifted to China and made a partner in the London firm of Bewick, Moreign, and Company. He then turned into a Henry James character, the American living abroad, the mining engineer of far-flung experiences and vast wealth, polished, cosmopolitan, a friend of the aristocracy, but maintaining intact within him his forefathers' dour faith in the humble virtues.

Mr. Hoover looks a patient and wise old man. He received me in the sitting room of his Waldorf-Astoria apartment, delicately painted gray, green, and ivory, and paneled in the Louis XV style which fashionable dressmakers and pastry shops prefer, the "style Faubourg" of nice people everywhere. The ex-President was dressed like an old banker, the soft collar just a little higher than necessary, still not as high as his old starched ones, the small feet encased in light English shoes, with tiny heels and arched insteps, like those in a Boldini portrait or those Edward VII used to wear. He spoke with quiet authority of his trips into a ghost world, which only he and a handful of scattered old men on both continents still remember, Russia under Czar Nicholas II, China under the last empress, Germany under Wilhelm II, Italy at the turn of the century, where he had been asked to conduct a geological and mineralogical survey.

As an old revolutionist, at the end of his life, feels himself usually closer to his former enemies, the people he hated and destroyed, than to his revolutionary successors, Mr. Hoover probably feels himself strangely attached to the vanished stage where he played the character of the disdainful American from the rude Far West, practical, ruthless, commanding, where he simplified problems in terms of time, money, plans, materials, and schedules.

Mr. Hoover is this, also: the Booth Tarkington businessman, who considers Europe with love and contempt as the victim of her own disregard for the practical facts of life, and the personification of the Americans' eternal desire to spread happiness and efficiency in the world. In Tientsin, during the Boxers' uprising, he organized the besieged concession, seized wheat stores, printed ration cards, built a temporary aqueduct, conquered a few cows grazing in no man's land to provide milk for the children and the sick, fortified the perimeter of his kingdom, while his wife served as a nurse with all the other women, in the improvised hospital. All this, of course, blossomed later into his First World War initiatives, bringing back stranded Americans from Europe, feeding children and old people on both sides, and, after the war, pouring food, medicines, raw materials, machinery into devastated areas, to prevent starving people from following the Russian and the Hungarian examples of bloody revolutions. His actions were dictated by his pioneer tradition, by his Quaker upbringing, and by his American inheritance. (His example was followed by Franklin Roosevelt with UNRRA and by Harry Truman with the Marshall Plan.)

In a sense, Mr. Hoover is both the ancestor who explains many curious traits in his descendants and the old man whose every idea is considered poison by later generations. I, as a foreigner, could look at him with the detachment of a historian, and saw only one difference between him and contemporary Americans: he never had thought he was renewing the world from its foundations with his initiatives.

Mr. Hoover was worried. There was no passion in his words but only the regretful tone of the doctor who names the disease which is killing a very dear patient. Can the United States alone shoulder all tasks, manufacture all the weapons, spend all the money, form the divisions, the sea and air fleets, defend all the frontiers menaced by Russia? Can the United States support the whole free world? Is the burden not too heavy?

He said, "The economic, political, and social repercus-

sions of our overambitious program are vast and dangerous. The dollar has been slipping for years. Inflation is
dangerous for us all, as all currencies in the free world
are anchored to ours. Inflation slowly changes the moral
basis on which we built our nation. I'll give you an example. In Iowa, ten per cent of the people who bought
farms recently did not intend working the land but
rented it to farmers. This had never happened before in
my native state. It's a new phenomenon, the rise of the
absentee landowner. There are other signs: people do
not want to save money any more and do not want to
make money. Last year 60,000 engineers graduated from
universities, this year 34,000, next year only 24,000.
Young people do not want to waste time to study difficult subjects and to take hard courses which take years,
cost a lot of money, and will lead them inevitably to executive jobs. Who wants an executive job? You work
more, you spoil your health, you miss the fine things of
life, and you have no longer the old hope of making a
fortune to leave your children. Now, I ask you, what
will happen to this mechanical, engineering civilization
of ours without engineers? How can you run such a
complex organization without technicians? The effort
which is being asked from the nation is too much for her
strength, economically and industrially. We are running
dangerously short of some raw materials while at the
same time the armament program lags behind schedule.

"An American soldier," Mr. Hoover continued, "costs
$10,000 a year to feed and lodge, without counting
equipment, arms, ammunition, transport, communica-

tion, instruction, and other incidental expenditures. Do you really believe we can guarantee the freedom of the world with American infantry? Should we not organize ourselves some other way? If Europe cannot do something for herself, I think Europe does not deserve to be saved.

"What we are doing," Mr. Hoover went on, "seems to be at the same time too much and not enough."

# V

*We must realize that size alone is not sufficient. The biggest force is not necessarily the best force.*

DWIGHT D. EISENHOWER

*This Nation cannot escape history.* ABRAHAM LINCOLN

THIS WAS THE FIRST KOREAN LESSON, then, that war is not an isolated incident but one of the many ways of conducting foreign policy, that war is the fruit of what came before and the generator of subsequent events. All this had been written by Clausewitz many years ago, of course.

It had been forgotten. Even during the Second World War, the Department of State was never kept informed of what the armed forces were thinking, as it was believed that diplomats and soldiers were doing different jobs. Cordell Hull confessed in his memoirs that the problem of where armies were to be landed and what itineraries they were to follow on the continent of Europe, in their grand strategy to defeat Hitler, had never been discussed with him either by the President or by his military advisers. All Americans now ought to know that the world they face was shaped by those very itineraries, by agreements of generals in the field. They all ought to know that armies are not very big fire brigades rushing to a conflagration by any route they think best.

Other conclusions (most of them ancient and forgotten truths) deduced from recent events were these:

—A Great Power's military preparation is a necessary sacrifice, like safety vaults in banks, not built for defense alone, but to deter possible hostile acts; it must always be proportioned to the Power's physical might, to its love of peace, international aims, the enemies which its policy provokes, and it must be prepared for the worst.

—Primitive men in vast hordes, thrown against modern men, brought up to trust machines, are dangerous because they still possess human resources of initiative, resistance, and resignation which modern men have been losing.

—There is no machine which can guarantee victory.

—Other people can make machines, too.

—It is not enough to be on the right side.

—There are wars in which one cannot concentrate all one has on the battlefield for one strong push and go home.

—It is not always true that one's allies are honorable people and one's enemies blood-drinking demons.

Above all, many Americans learned that the United States can no longer rest on its capacity to generate avalanches of arms and machines and to mobilize millions of men, because, this time, no matter how many divisions it can muster and how many factories it can convert, there will never be enough. The problem of peace cannot be solved with money and steel alone. Abundance is no longer sufficient.

It now appears that the Korean aggression was perhaps the gravest mistake the communists could have made. Until then the United States had really lived in the illusion that her traditional policy could be resumed, that the world could be patched up with a few billion dollars and a few well-worded and noble treaties. Until then Americans still put all their hopes in new, miraculous gadgets, the magic weapons which would have destroyed the enemy wherever he was, and which made it unnecessary for men to dig holes in the mud, to eat food out of tins, to plunge bayonets in other men's bellies, and to die in the mine fields or on barbed-wire entanglements.

These recent lessons, however, are so contrary to the Americans' traditions and hopes that it is difficult for a foreigner to assess how deep they have penetrated into common consciousness and how much they have modified the thoughts of generals and politicians.

"We really learned nothing new in Korea," said Colonel J.S.W., looking at the ashes of his cigar. The other officers around the table nodded. The colonel was in command of one of the first battalions to rush to the front, a battalion which during the first heroic weeks of the war was wiped out and re-formed several times. He

was wounded by mortar shell fragments, promoted, and
assigned to the Infantry School, Fort Benning, Georgia,
to lecture on his experiences.

"We really learned nothing new in Korea," he went
on. "We've been reminded of many old things which we
had known and forgotten."

I had asked the question: "What did you learn in Korea?" A few days before, in the Pentagon, speaking with
staff officers, I had been told repeatedly that "there are
no sure systems to win wars," that "war is war, as the
French say," and that "we don't put all our hopes in one
new weapon to give us victory." Other experts had told
me that "nobody thinks any more of a push-button war"
and that the production of normal, ordinary weapons
was being pushed together with research and experimenting on wonder weapons, as "nothing can take their
place on the battlefield today." All this had not completely reassured me. I had not quite believed my ears.
It was as incredible as if I had heard an American say
that sailing ships were still splendid means for crossing
the Atlantic, or that stagecoaches could assure good
communications from city to city. Had the military become less American than the American people? When I
visited Fort Benning, I took the opportunity to question
an expert, Colonel W., the Korean veteran.

Colonel W. spoke fluently, for the things he was explaining to me were obviously the same he taught in the
classroom. He explained that perhaps the United States
had made some political blunders in Korea, due to its
good faith and generous attitude, but not military errors,

because all the difficulties in the beginning had not come from a faulty use of men and weapons but from their scarcity. The men had fought well, even in those first disastrous weeks, and had showed great capacity to learn quickly a new kind of war. It was the worst kind of war for American infantrymen, a war in the mountains, with no road communications, in which tanks were used as artillery and not as cavalry weapons. On the other hand, it was a mistake to think that it was an old-fashioned war, as all the modern appliances and machines were being fully employed. Still, those first few weeks taught everybody that machines alone could not conquer and defend terrain. The colonel said, "the most powerful armored vehicle is no stronger than the men inside."

This, the colonel confessed, was old stuff, still it was more and more difficult to explain it to new soldiers and officers who came from a civilian life in which the hope of a scientific miracle is unconscious and general. These men, the colonel said, read science fiction. They look at interplanetary rockets on television. They read the spaceship comic books. Military problems in popular magazines are always treated on the same super-mechanical level. It was even more necessary now to keep on training infantrymen along the same old-fashioned lines, because they had, of course, to learn the use of the many modern weapons and machines. But above all they must not forget the virtues of the old foot soldiers, the virtues of American soldiers of all times: the will to win, adaptability, initiative, courage, resistance, intelligent use of the situation, the terrain and the momentary advantages. To reconcile these two things, the confidence in machines and reliance on man's innate moral qualities, was not as simple as it looked, because they seemed contradictory to many young men. "When too much hope is put on machinery," said the colonel, "and things go bad, morale may break more easily."

Early one morning, in Fort Benning, we went to see an infantry battalion attacking a few low hills covered with yellow stubble and surrounded by a sea of low pine trees. The men were to demonstrate the use of all the latest and the older weapons a typical battalion carries into battle today for the advantage of a group of European journalists and American businessmen. In front of a makeshift tribune an officer stood, his back to the show, and talked into a chest microphone. His timing was that of an orchestra conductor. When he said, "Now, on your right you'll see some F84s which will drop napalm bombs against target A," he did not turn around to see whether his words had been followed by the action. The planes, tanks, men appeared always when, and as, he described them and did exactly what he had said. Sometimes he switched the public-address system to the radio-telephones over which the many commanders on the field directed the operation, and we could hear the orders given, discussed, explained, accepted, the co-ordination of the various movements. It was, of course, a well-drilled peacetime maneuver; I had never seen anything of the kind so impeccably conducted, as there are usually many little differences between plans and execution, in the best of armies, planes a little late, tanks slow in moving, men too eager to get to the objective, which make continuous adjustments necessary. Things, of course, never come off that smoothly in war.

We saw the artillery barrage, the men shooting recoilless rifles, bazookas, machine guns, mortars, and all sorts of other explosives toward three yellow hills. Then the tanks went into action, shooting away at the target, and the planes swooped low, dropping incendiary bombs or shooting rockets. Finally the men came out of their holes and started creeping toward the top of the hills hurling hand grenades and shooting all the portable weapons issued to them. The amount of noise, smoke, and dust concentrated into a few hundred yards was incredible. It was easy to believe that no human being could stay alive long, there, even if buried under the earth or concrete fortifications. When the men reached the enemy positions silence suddenly fell and we again heard our voices speaking with our neighbors. The smoke and dust slowly cleared with the breeze.

I was not greatly surprised at the immense quantity of explosives the infantrymen and all supporting units could concentrate on the targets within a few minutes. It was double the fire power of a similar battalion during World War II, I was told. What puzzled me was the great variety of weapons, the great variety of calibers for similar weapons, and the great variety of projectiles which could be shot from one single weapon. It seemed a strangely un-American way of doing things, for have Americans not always sought to simplify, standardize, unify all sorts of things, in order to streamline problems? Because, I thought, the principal question was no longer how much could that battalion shoot, how many weapons could the men carry with them in combat, how many the supporting units could train on targets, but the vital problem now was how much ammunition could the supply system bring to the firing line. Obviously, in actual war, that battalion would rarely have the fire power the organizational charts assigned it and which we saw demonstrated in front of us, but only what the transport units accumulated in a given time, at a given spot, under actual fighting conditions, in whatever terrain the men happened to operate.

Maximum offensive power, in any army, requires such a number of favorable circumstances that it can only be fully developed in peacetime training exhibitions. In this case, however, the requirements for a normal performance seemed especially heavy: in order to maintain a twenty-four-hours-a-day flow of trucks you need a plain in the back of the fighting line, efficient roads kept in good repair, railroads, bridges, and complete air supremacy everywhere at all times. Should one of these requirements fail, the power of the fighting units would fade. What would happen, for instance, if the battalion were on irregular ground, not easily reached by trucks, or if it were traveling fast in the pursuit of a beaten enemy? How could it be kept supplied with the variety of ammunition of all calibers it needed and the scientific food, refinements, and comforts which seem to be indispensable to American fighting men? What would happen if the air supremacy were lost even for a short time or had to be defended?

Truly, I assured myself, battle conditions are seldom as bad as one imagines them, an over-armed battalion always has a better chance of fighting on, even when most of its power is annulled, than an under-armed battalion, for it is better to *abundare quam deficere*. It is also true, I assured myself, that roads can be built quickly with earth-moving machinery, or, as at Montecassino and in Korea, mule trains can be improvised and coolies can be recruited. Furthermore, American ingenuity has invented many new ways of supplying isolated troops: helicopters, slow transport planes which can land on small emergency strips or drop cases of ammunition, food, vehicles, and guns from the sky. On the other hand, all these things, the mule trains, the coolies, the helicopters, the transport planes, are no better than makeshift *ersatz* for massive road transport, stopgap remedies for dramatic circumstances. No real organization can be built solely on them. No long and mobile offensive can be fed by such means. Men and animals slowly carry a small amount and sometimes take weeks to build up a few days' fire power. Helicopters and transport planes are easy targets and can be shot down like clay pigeons.

I imagined myself the commander of that very battalion, facing a difficult enemy, far from the roads, on mountain tops, the day after a big fight, when communication lines have to be re-established, supplies are short, and positions must be fortified and defended at all costs. I shuddered at the size of my problem, at the danger of being short of vital material or oversupplied with something I did not need. I talked about this with the officers assigned to us, but they seemed not to worry. They were extremely and justly proud of the amount of explosive which could be hurled against the enemy by relatively few men, they illustrated each weapon, which was either new or redesigned with great improvements, some of them dictated by actual fighting conditions, battle-tested in Korea, explained that the shells were the last word in technical perfection and engineering skill, and the men were well trained to use and maintain each weapon and device. "These men," said a captain, "are accustomed from civilian life to handle machinery. There's very little we can teach them. This is the Western soldier's great superiority over the raw, ignorant, and unskilled communist. This we must exploit as much as we can."

What I had seen, of course, was not a military demonstration but only a show prepared to impress and entertain visitors from abroad and American businessmen. I was not supposed to draw final conclusions from it. On the other hand, it was extremely difficult not to notice the emphasis which was being put on certain things and the pride of the officers in charge. Doubts and theoretical thinking are naturally never encouraged at their level. Captains and majors in any army are not supposed to think in terms of army corps and organizational charts. Still, some of them must have known that there was a law of diminishing returns, a point where the mere addition of a pistol might decrease the unit's over-all offensive capacity instead of increasing it. To add anything beyond that point sometimes may not be a purely military decision. It becomes a symbolic, superstitious, magical gesture, as if recoilless rifles, infra-red gunsights, or vitamin pills were no longer considered means to defeat the enemy but fetishes, amulets, charms, endowed with supernatural powers of their own, like the gods which the ancient Romans brought to battle with them. I asked myself if that point had been reached.

At Fort Knox I saw the new, flat, powerful tanks maneuvering at great speed in the vast reservation, new armored warfare techniques skillfully taught to men of all nationalities, and secret experimental models, which were being improved for final design and mass production. Here Americans were at their ease. Here were great ingenious machines, skillfully contrived, incorporating all imaginable devices and scientific aids for smooth performance on the battlefield. There was even a little telephone which looked strangely homelike on the outside of the armor for the infantrymen to talk to the crew locked inside under fire. I was told that an in-

fantry division has today more tanks than many tank
divisions during World War II and that the difference
between the infantry division and the armored division
is only in the number of tanks and the tactics employed:
an infantry division sends the men ahead and protects
them with the tanks' supporting fire, an armored division sends the tanks ahead and the men behind to mop
up. Technically, both could easily be considered armored divisions.

Here again, as at Fort Benning, the emphasis was on
quantity of material, number of vehicles, power of motors, speed, capacity to fire rapidly any number of specialized shells, and very modern scientific devices. Here,
again, nothing was said about the supply problem, the
technique which had undoubtedly been evolved to feed
the steel monsters and the men with everything they
needed while driving on.

From all this—the infantry battalion demonstration
and the visit to Fort Knox—it became clear that the new
United States divisions, the most powerful in the history
of man, can be most effective only under particular circumstances. Its very massive weight makes it a none
too flexible instrument. United States Army units must
inevitably fight best as they advance, against a slowly
retreating enemy, in great plains rich with easy communications, under complete air protection. The heavy
armament, the extremely complex supply problem, the
design of the armored vehicles, made for great speed in
open country, the large number of tanks assigned to
each infantry division would make a war on broken

or mountainous terrain an extremely difficult one. The stores at the back of each fighting unit must necessarily be at all times of such magnitude that an elastic maneuver would almost be impossible. The men could seldom *reculer pour mieux sauter*, or quickly shift their position to reinforce a dangerous spot in the line. Any movement that was not a slow advance would endanger them, their supplies and their offensive capacity.

If the United States Army staff were Prussian or French, trained to rigorous logic, it would be easy to conclude that the war for which they are preparing, the only war at which they can deploy all their might, is the war they plan, the war they will make. The plains of Germany and Poland are among the few spots in the world which present the ideal terrain for great armored offensives and the communication system for massive supplying. When would this prefabricated war come? Obviously as soon as the air and land superiority has been reached (the enemy, as we have seen, must slowly retreat and must not even be able to dispute the command of the air), and not before the weapons which are now being mass-produced become obsolete. That would bring the date within the next five, six or seven years.

The United States general staff is not, however, recruited from abstract thinkers. They are practical men. It may be that the war we have deduced from their armament and tactics will be the war they would prefer to fight or the war history will make them fight. On the other hand, it is impossible to say whether, like Prussians or French, they have pushed their military imagi-

nation so far ahead or whether they have built a rigorous bridge of theoretical conclusions chained one to
another. It may be that staff officers have worked earnestly and hard, like collectors gathering rare speci-
mens, to add all the latest inventions to the armed forces,
to leave no scientific stone unturned, while tirelessly
improving the older weapons and discarding what was
impractical, without stopping to consider the over-all
picture or trying to figure out at what point the coral-
like accumulation of new arms, specialized foods, and
novel devices stopped strengthening a fighting unit, and
when exactly began the danger of weakening it.

It is extremely difficult to know. No American ever
talks in abstract terms. Even deep-thinking Americans,
people who must delve into the realm of general ideas,
never talk freely about them. Theoretical thinking probably seems to them a shameful weakness, which they
must hide at all costs, as it sets them apart from their
fellow countrymen. This, however, I could say. Americans, in those branches of human activity I know
something about, mostly concentrate on concrete details, which they tirelessly improve and polish to perfection, worrying little about the broad principles at the
back of their work and of whose existence they are only
reluctantly aware. Their love of novelty, progress, science is mostly conservative. They devise automatic,
self-adjusting, thermostat-controlled, streamlined coffee-
pots, but apparently give little thought to what, for
continental Europeans, is the fundamental problem, the
taste of the final product. They adopt new lenses, new

films, new three-dimensional techniques, new color processes, new, elaborate ways to build sets, to tell an old
film story.

The best one can say is that the reliance on pure abundance and scientific improvements has undoubtedly
strengthened the United States armed forces beyond
what was imagined possible a few years ago but has, at
the same time, limited their scope and narrowed their
capacity to make war under all circumstances. Whether
this is a conscious or unconscious process may be irrelevant, as the war Americans prepare for and try to prevent is, after all, the war at which they would be best,
war in the great plains of Western Europe against an
enemy who has been trained mostly to advance or to
retreat slowly and not to shift swiftly about. This spe-
cialization may have little practical consequences but
definite psychological repercussions on American foreign policy. A threat to Western Germany, the chance
to attack Poland or the Ukraine, for instance, will necessarily be considered by the Pentagon within a few
years with different eyes than the defense of the mountainous and impervious borders of Turkey, Iran or India, as the man who only owns tropical clothes will
unconsciously seek chances to travel south and will avoid,
if possible, going in the other direction. The temptation
to choose the time and the terrain in which to deploy
all their advantages will be unavoidable. Whether the
United States will yield to it or not is another question.

# VI

*Le bon sens suffit au train ordinaire de la société; et chez un peuple dont l'éducation est faite, la liberté démocratique appliquée aux affaires intérieures de l'Etat produit plus de bien que les erreurs du gouvernement de la démocratie ne sauraient amener de maux. Mais il n'est pas toujours ainsi dans les rapports de peuple à peuple. La politique extérieure n'exige l'usage de presque aucune des qualités qui sont propres à la démocratie, et commande au contraire le développement de presque toutes celles qui lui manquent.* ALEXIS DE TOCQUEVILLE

A STRANGE PERPLEXITY seems to corrode the bold assurance of the American people, as if, by different roads, through different experiences, for sometimes contradictory reasons, they had all arrived at the same dead end, the old people in Los Angeles bored with mechanical comforts, the inventor who hopefully pursues nature's elusive secrets, the State Department officials who endlessly dig the quarry of mimeographed facts, the staff officers who test and adopt new wonderful weapons.

It is as if everybody realized that the rainbow ends nowhere and there is no pot of gold to be found. Per-

haps one of the most obvious examples of this contradictory aspect of American life is the New York traffic.
For more than half a century, every resource of United
States industry, billions of dollars, human lives, endless
research, patience, and ingenuity have been dedicated to
producing more and more cars, faster, cheaper, more
powerful models, with the final result that in New York
everybody walks. Another example which foreigners
notice is the elephantiasis of American newspapers. Such
is the publishers' wealth and power, who can make use
of so many modern devices for gathering and printing
news, opinions, pictures, cartoons (the best correspondents everywhere, telecommunications of all kinds, river-
like delivery of mass agency news, syndicated features
of all quality, taste, and weight, fast machinery to print
mountains of copies an hour), such is also the wealth of
the market and the abundance of advertising, that newspapers have become unwieldy paper mattresses, impen-
etrable jungles, filled with overlong and overdetailed
news stories, some of which are extremely good but lost
in a confusion of brassieres, corsets, candies, mink coats,
television sets and new automobiles.

Only an experienced reader can cut his way to the
things he wants. Newcomers are easily lost. This, in the
country which believes itself to worship the practical,
the concise, the predigested, the timesaving in everything. Or take American popular magazines which have
reached such technical perfection and such large circula-
tions that they must be planned, written, illustrated, and
made up many months before publication. Christmas

scenes are painted by sweating artists in the summer, bathing-suited models shiver in January beach scenes. All contents are as old the day they appear as those in magazines which used to be found in dentists' waiting rooms in the days when publishing speed was practically unknown. Another illustration of the same contradictions is the American scientists' complaints (which one sees often in magazines or hears from their own voices) who have discovered that funds, large laboratories, well-paid and competent staffs seldom uncover great truths, because all the important discoveries still seem to be made by solitary workers pursuing fixed ideas in their dingy little laboratories, with practically no staff and little money.

The dead end is the discovery, which everyone makes sooner or later, that abundance is not enough. Nothing, of course, can be done without adequate means. The solitary scientist must have time, some laboratory space and enough money for his requirements. But means are not enough to reach the goal. There is no way to buy success, certainty, truth and peace. There is no way to build a foolproof word machine, supplied with the latest accessories, automatic pacts, clauses, agreements, to prevent war. There is no way to fight a war with machines, even very expensive machines, without getting killed. Abundance not only solves few problems but makes them all more complicated and obscure, as extremely rich men have discovered who tried to live human and pleasant lives. It was easier to edit a newspaper when one had not too much copy. It was easier to make a good picture when technical means were few and budgets were low. It was easier to shape a foreign policy when one did not have limitless means and when one trimmed one's ambitions to the size of one's power. This discovery casts a shadow over the life of everyone, in the United States, whether they are conscious of it or not. One often hears friends recall how beautiful and hopeful the world was years ago when they could still believe they were on the threshold of a new happy era when all man's problems were to vanish like ghosts at the stroke of midnight.

The United States is still filled with the same old books that teach everything: how to make love, how to make friends, how to dress with style, how to write a novel, a play, a film script, a short story, how to get fat or thin, how to tap one's secret sources of energy, how to cure all diseases with faith, diets, massages, or confessions. Girls still buy the many books that teach them to acquire charm and beauty through will power, I was told by a clerk in a Grand Central Station bookstore, but most of them now know that the chances of changing their appearance or their personality are slim, as the commuters who buy guides to gardening know that they will never grow the cabbagelike flowers shown in the illustrations. "The girls now know," he said, "that the woman who studied how to enter a room with poise and grace, as shown in Chapter One, will probably stumble on the carpet, overturn a table, and pour tomato juice on her dress. The girl who wants to be charming at all costs possibly may be avoided like poison."

The same sadness of the defeated gardener and the ugly girl can be felt in the words of the editors of *Fortune* who wrote a book, which was widely distributed by the United States Information Service, called *U.S.A. The Permanent Revolution:* "What is the aim of our propaganda? Friendship? To many Americans this is the end-all. And nothing has done us more grievous harm— for we are offended terribly when love is not forthcoming from others. It is quite impossible anyway. We have only to look at India; since their departure, the British, who never gave a damn whether anybody liked them or not, have become increasingly popular, while we, who did our best to expedite that departure, are becoming increasingly unpopular."

Love blossoms unjustly in the garden of the British who did not buy the book on "how to do it," and love avoids that of the Americans.

This, I think, is the American crisis, the setting of a wonderful certainty. The dream of a better future is always there to warm the heart: the dream of a peaceful, just, healthy, well-fed, free, rich, brotherly world, which somehow should be generated by their sacrifices, sorrow, and blood; but it is no more than a dream now, in which people are sometimes afraid to believe, whereas before it was a concrete itinerary and a timetable for history. There are things which technique, money, abundance, research, diligence alone do not change. Perhaps old man Kettering secretly suspects that without books or a new philosophy he will never discover the secret of why the grass is green. President Eisenhower now knows that aid to foreign countries, no matter how abundant, will not defeat Russia. Arthur Sulzberger now knows that the New York *Times* cannot really contain all the news that is fit to print. Doctor Gallup now knows that there is no way to find out exactly what people will do in the future. The old beacons of American life are burning dimly. The old guideposts cannot be trusted any more. But were they the only beacons and the only guideposts?

In 1929 there was a gray, Gothic church being built in one of the most visible points in Manhattan, and I was sent to interview the minister in charge of planning and construction. He said to me, "This, my boy, is a twenty-million-dollar answer to materialism." There was sadness in his voice. I remember his ironical smile and the little gesture which embraced the twenty million dollars, the contemporary materialism, the great American pride in figures and concrete achievement, but also the church, the secret desire to atone, to preserve something of the ancestors' faith, to sacrifice humbly what one had held dearest.

"We Americans are strangely ashamed to command," said M.K., a childhood friend who has now lived in Lon-

don for many years. "When I came to Europe the first
time I found myself unable to behave as my servants
wanted me to. I always asked their opinions—not to
feel alone, perhaps, or to be comforted by their experience—and often I did things for myself, when the maid
was away, not to have to go through the effort of giving orders. Did you ever notice that servants in many
houses of Americans living in Europe or the East are not
happy and behave badly? It may be due to our democratic education, our repugnance to consider anybody
an inferior, but then it may also be due to our fear of
not being loved, the fear of some sort of responsibility.
Some friends of mine treat their children with apparent
fear, as if the children held some strange power over
them. Americans are also bad at training animals. Lion
tamers are mostly foreigners in American circuses. This
you must remember when you try to judge the American capacity for leadership."

T. S. McD., who fought the war in the high echelons
of command, said to me once, "In order to give orders,
to plan ahead, to decide anything, there must be many
of us. We want to have the warm feeling of moving as
a group and to be comforted by the opinions of all the
others. We want to share responsibilities. Then we feel
we are invincible. This, mind you, has not always been
true of Americans. In older days, lonely men who took
on themselves enormous burdens were admired and im-
itated. It is relatively new. We love to gather around tables with memo pads and pencils. We love to exchange

mimeographed documents in many copies, to be returned with comments when read. We seem to fear that history may later pin one name, and one name alone, to a decision. Have you ever tried to find a man, in Washington, or in Wall Street, or anywhere, who is really responsible for a given matter or who can give assurances or whose word you can count on? It's almost impossible. That's why individuals, in the United States, feel so free from restraint. They know they don't count."

Gino Tomaiuoli, veteran Italian correspondent in Washington, said to me, "It is difficult to assess the real meaning of the Americans' faith in quantity and mechanical organization. In part, they naturally rely on the technique which has allowed them to do many incredible things in the past. Then, it may also cover a certain amount of doubt and fear. Americans are sometimes naturally baffled by a complicated and hostile world. They often don't understand it and they don't know how to prod it in the right direction. It reacts, moves, lives and dies for reasons which mostly escape them. In difficult and dangerous moments, it is inevitable that they should cling to their old formulas, which give them the reassuring feeling that, no matter how badly things turn out, they have Aladdin's lamp, for they know an expensive yet one-hundred-per-cent certain system to get results, any result, whether breaking through Hitler's Atlantic wall, stopping revolution anywhere anytime, or defeating communism."

A spiritual crisis in the United States, in the years to come, would mean the end of the Western World. Peace has been sustained by American moral and industrial strength to such a point that the name of the pact which defends it should be derived not from the ocean but from Atlas who supported the weight of the universe on his shoulders.

Until now, the crisis did not yet look like a dangerous one. Americans are beginning to be a little wary of excessive hopes. They try to shun, as President Eisenhower said, "not only the crude counsel of despair but also the self-deceit of easy illusions." At the same time, they still want to believe that all problems can be solved their traditional way: that a strong Europe will inevitably range herself and fight for the common civilization, that a rearmed Japan will be a United States sentry in the Far East, just as they believed, at one time, that all Germans would willingly don a uniform to defend the Elbe. Americans still have confidence that nobody seriously questions their love for fellow human beings and their disinterestedness, and they still think there must be a sure way out of the present nightmare if only one knew what arrows to follow.

Their very optimism, however, may be dangerous, as it may turn any day into despair. The crisis would have two faces. Americans suddenly could believe that nothing, no new weapon, no new policy, or new foreign-aid appropriation, will really avert the dangers they face and that there is no possible stable settlement of the world's troubles. As a consequence they might restrict their efforts to what they know well, their own country, prepare to defend it like a last outpost and abandon the rest of us. In that case the free world will be doomed.

On the other hand, they may just as easily be persuaded that what the situation needs is more of the same treatment, and they may be tempted to bleed themselves to death, destroy their own liberties, accept totalitarian discipline, police control and censorship, in order to last and to bear the increasing burdens, and in the hope of seeing them diminish in the future. That day, again, the free world would be lost.

There are indications of both these aspects of the American crisis in the contemporary scene. They both have names. The free world would be doomed even today, when things still look hopeful and war is not imminent, if it were true that our common heritage could be defended with the facile philosophy of technical achievements and industrial abundance alone, that the final blossom of our civilization is merely that, mass production and new inventions, and that there is nothing else to defend. Sometimes, reading the obscure and badly translated pronouncements of lesser American politicians, Europeans are afraid that this may be true today, that the end has come and that the United States plan is going to defend only her own material conquests by allowing some, but not too much, prosperity to others, provided that they be willing also to fight and die in the common cause.

In other words the free world would be lost today if the United States were the country Americans usually describe and of which they often boast or if her strength were only the "know-how," the purely technical knowledge, and the American "way of life" what we see in Hollywood pictures and in cheaper magazines—mechanized hedonism, worship of the latest model, the chromium-plated, the streamlined, the homogenized, the vitaminized, the self-regulating, automatic and thermostat-controlled.

But is the United States really all that and nothing more? What is the United States? Is she really the eighteenth-century Utopia she wants to appear and which covers a multitude of ancient sins? A nation of experimenters without past, who have to invent everything anew, who must be the Adam, the Christ, the Plato, the Machiavelli, the Clausewitz of every new generation? Or is the United States a new civilization, born from our own, which is really on the verge of reaching a new form of brotherly relationship among men? Is it a world in which scientific progress has really freed men from ancient dooms? Is it a new empire which we do not understand because it has learned from our errors and does not employ the trite old rules which we and Metternich could understand, but on the contrary is finding its own, new, humane, civilized rules? On which side is America? Is it the last backwash of our own civilization or is it a new way of conceiving the world, man in it, his duties and rights?

This, after all is said, seemed to be the only question worth asking: "What is the United States?" because the answer was our common future. The course of history will be shaped not by elections, day-by-day votes of Congress, decisions of White House, Pentagon, or State Department officials, but by the secret logic with which people follow their course to the ultimate end, which is determined not by their conscious will but by their past, their faith, and their very being. The outcome of the struggle with communism depends entirely on what threat communism really represents to America. What are Americans afraid for?

I asked many people the same question. Monsignor William J. McDonald, who teaches philosophy at Washington's Catholic University, said to me, "It is difficult to know what Americans are, because they themselves do not know. They like to deceive themselves. They think and describe themselves as pragmatists, empiricists, relativists, and say they do not obey general rules but technical requirements. Of course, they are nothing of the kind. At Pearl Harbor and in Korea they discovered that they were ready to fight for reasons which were not pragmatic, empirical, and relativist, but much older than our own nation. They never mention them. They

prefer to demonstrate 'truth' with statistics, new mechanisms, graphs, maps, and other creations of the devil.
They did not like the Japanese, the Nazis, the Politburo,
in spite of the fact that these people were the real pragmatists, empiricists, and relativists. As a joke I often ask
friends their definition of the 'American way of life' but
I never get a satisfactory answer. Still, it is the idea for
which we are all ready to die. Sometimes, for the sake
of argument, I ask whether gangsters, Reno divorces,
lynchings, political corruption—all of which are to be
found within the borders of our country, generated by
our past history—are part of the inheritance we defend.
They all deny it with horror. What then? I remember
the advice which G. K. Chesterton gave the boarding-
house keeper, to find out not whether a new boarder
had money but what his philosophy and his religion
were, because only from them could she find out
whether he would pay his rent regularly and preserve
the furniture with care."

This general confusion is increased by the fact that
in the United States one never distinguishes the purpose
for which Americans busy themselves from the technique they employ, the "know-how" from the "know-
why," the goal of the trip from the vehicle. The real,
deep, unconscious motives are never analyzed. Prime
Minister Louis Stephen St. Laurent of Canada told a
friend of mine months ago the following anecdote
which could serve as an illustration. He was the guest of
President Truman and, talking informally with him, told
him, "Sometimes, at night, I cannot sleep when I think

of my responsibilities. The idea of how many human lives can be affected by my decisions troubles me." Harry Truman answered, "I sleep very well. When I have some important decision to take, I ask myself, 'What is right and what is wrong?' And I make up my mind to do what I believe is right."

Harry Truman, like all good politicians, was thinking aloud the thoughts of the majority of his people. His way of determining the right course to follow was probably the only one that assured him the approval of the multitudes. After having examined the experts' opinions, the Department of State memorandums, the poll results, after having listened to his Cabinet, influential congressmen and his staff, he would ultimately consult a lone man, a middle-aged Missouri politician, born on a farm, a veteran of the First World War, who had read Plutarch and the Bible in his youth and liked to quote from both, a man like many in the United States, Harry Truman, and took his decisions not as a scientific Superman but as the Christian, Protestant, American farmer he was—right or wrong—on the basis of the philosophy which he had unconsciously inherited from his ancestors, more complex than all the empirical deviltries devised by modern experts. His simple guide was the same Chesterton had suggested to his boarding-house keeper.

This must be remembered: Americans are often the worst interpreters of themselves because they only think of an imaginary country, the mechanical paradise which they would like it to be, and they forget that the United States is also an ancient European nation. Morally, if not geographically, she could be placed in the North Sea, with borders touching Great Britain, Normandy, Belgium, Holland, Germany and the Scandinavian countries, with a long tail reaching to the Mediterranean, where the California vineyards and the sun-baked plains of the Southwest could find room.

It was easy to forget years ago that the United States was also a European country when history proceeded peacefully, everybody believed in progress, and everything that was old was to be discarded or neglected for the new. Now that many Americans have reached a dead end, and the old simple rules have shown themselves to be useful but insufficient, they are looking for some new assurance, for new guides, and they will remember that they are part of a vaster world and that they have never really broken away from an experience which goes back many centuries. What set them apart from the rest of the world was important yesterday. What seems important today, on the other hand, is what is common to all of us. Increasingly, Americans discover that the very complex and frightening problems they are facing have been faced by other men in other ages and that speed, machines, power, scientific progress, have not changed the deep essence of things.

In the smoking compartments of great trains, in the airport waiting rooms, at a Rotary lunch in Anniston,

Alabama, at dinner in a Detroit restaurant, at breakfast in Beverly Hills; in talking with officers in military bases, with students, journalists, businessmen, or plain, ordinary, unknown people in bars, I kept on hearing the same idea, said with the same words, as if the same thought had blossomed in everybody's head. The sentence, which sooner or later, inevitably, appeared in the conversation, is "We must get back to fundamentals." It is usually said with a virile tone, as if the speaker had awakened from a dream in time to save himself from ruin. Sometimes it is pronounced with a baffled and perplexed tone like an invocation to a saint. The sentence is usually brought out when talking of international affairs, Soviet Russia, Europe, Korea, but it is mentioned also when discussing everyday, ordinary things. "Fundamentals" may mean almost everything, a more sober view of future possibilities, but also love for one woman, death, virile bringing up of children, simple pleasures which must not be sacrificed to the desire for wealth and success or the moral significance of life.

The "return to fundamentals" may mean the return to the homely hopes of the ancestors, the sober discipline of older days, the spirit of sacrifice. Even Western moving pictures now seem to probe the same problem. Many are unusually serious and seem to ask, "Who are we, and why did we drive so many miles across the continent, fighting Indians, cutting down forests and building homesteads?"

"Americana" of all kinds fascinate the public: books of ancient and naive prints, photographs of the Civil

War, real or imitation antiques, folk songs, folk dances. Nowhere else in the world are people so keenly interested in themselves and in their past. Italians publish no popular illustrated books about their past history, write no historical novels about the *Risorgimento*, worry very little when they destroy historical landmarks, glorious *palazzi*, or raze crooked medieval streets to erect flimsy Latin American reinforced concrete monstrosities on a new, straight avenue. The old explanation that Americans worship their history because they have little of it is worthless. They had even less history in years gone by; still they never paid as much attention to it as they do now. It also must not be forgotten that the United States is, today, one of the oldest unchanged nations existing, and that her form of government is the oldest after the British and the Vatican, so that the pretense of her perennial youth is absurd.

It is a surprising discovery, this new absorbing interest. Senator Alexander Wiley of Wisconsin was looking at a copy of Thucydides in his senate office, when I went to visit him, months ago. The Senator is a cordial, kindly, optimistic man, jealous guardian of the cheese-manufacturing interests of his home state and not usually dedicated to the perusal of the classics. He was reading Pericles' funeral oration when I went in. "Listen to this," he said. "It sounds as if it had been written today for us." And he read the well-known passage: "Our constitution does not copy the laws of neighboring states . . . Its administration favors the many instead of the few: this is why it is called democracy . . . The laws afford equal justice to all in their private differences . . . Advancement in public life falls to reputation for capacity, class considerations not being allowed to interfere with merit, nor again does poverty bar the way. If a man is able to serve the State, he is not hindered by the obscurity of his conditions . . . We do not feel angry with our neighbor for doing what he likes . . . But all this in our private relations does not make us lawless as citizens . . . We provide plenty of means for the mind to refresh itself from business. We celebrate games and sacrifices all year around. The magnitude of our city draws the produce of the world into our harbor so that to the Athenian the fruits of other countries are as familiar a luxury as those of his own . . . We throw open our city to the world and never by alien acts exclude foreigners from any opportunity of learning and observing, although the eyes of an enemy may occasionally profit by our liberality, trusting less in system and policy than to the native spirit of our citizens. Where our rivals from their very cradles, by a painful discipline, seek after manliness, at Athens we live exactly as we please and yet are just as ready to encounter every legitimate danger . . . We have the double advantage of escaping the experience of hardships in anticipation and of facing them in the hour of need as fearlessly as those who are never free from them . . . We cultivate refinements without extravagance and knowledge without effeminacy. Wealth we employ more for use than for show and place the real disgrace of poverty not in owning to the fact but in declining to struggle against it."

Thucydides, with his facile parallel between democracy and the totalitarian, militarized state, is read today by unsuspected people. A young man who sat next to me in the plane between New York and Chicago quoted several passages by heart. He was employed by the Johnson and Johnson Company and was on his way to Wisconsin to see whether cheese manufacturers were interested in a new material his organization had developed to use in bandages and which could just as easily be employed in the packaging of delicate merchandise. A quotation from Thucydides, on courage being generated by confidence and confidence by long practice, is on the door of the Navy Submarine School in New London. Captain Charles Triebel, Commander, said to me, "It's as if it had been written by one of us."

Even James Forrestal's thoughts turned to the ancients the night he died. The last words he had written were from William Praed's translation of Sophocles' *Ajax:*

*Fair Salamis, the billows' roar*
 *Wanders around thee yet;*
*And sailors gaze upon thy shore*
 *Firm in the ocean set.*

The Container Corporation of America buys magazine pages to praise not its products but "Great Ideas of Western Man." A recent advertisement was dedicated to Montesquieu "on the nature of liberty." "Political liberty does not consist in an unlimited freedom . . . We must have continually present to our minds the difference between independence and liberty. Liberty is a right of doing whatever the laws permit, and if a citizen could do what they forbid, he would no longer be possessed of liberty, because all his fellow citizens would have the same power."

The United States Catholic Bishops' minds returned to the end of the Roman Empire, in November, 1951, when they prepared a letter to all American citizens.

"An alarming parallel exists between the situation facing us today and that which faced the Roman Empire 1500 years ago," they wrote. "The problems of the Empire closely resemble those which sorely test us now— barbarism on the outside, refined materialism and moral decay within. Confronted by those problems, what were men of that time concerned with? St. Augustine, who lived in that period, gives us the answer in a memorable passage, 'They do not trouble about the moral degradation of the Empire. All that they ask is that it should be prosperous and secure. What concerns us (they say) is that everyone should be able to increase his wealth so that he can afford lavish expenditure and can keep the weak in subjection. Let the laws protect the rights of property and let them leave man's morals alone . . . Let there be sumptuous banquets where anybody can play and drink and gorge himself and be dissipated by day or night as much as he pleases or is able. Let the noise of dancing be everywhere and let the theatres resound with lewd merriment . . . Let the man who dislikes these pleasures be regarded as a public enemy.' "

All this would probably pass unnoticed were it not for the fact that nobody in Europe, not intellectuals, clergymen, nor corporations, turns to the ancient texts in the hope of illuminating the way. Of course, quotations can be found everywhere. The critic will adorn his prose with a line or two from a lesser poet, the priest will embellish his sermon with a sprig of holy prose and the statesman will lard his speech with the words of his predecessors. All this is ornamentation or the pleasure of finding one's own ideas confirmed by some dead thinker.

It is a different matter, in the United States. There is the surprise of discovering that men have long ago battled against the very problems which frighten the world today and that the ancients' experience can be used as a guide. St. Augustine, for instance, is not quoted on some fine point of doctrine as one of the Doctors of the Church, but only as a wise man who has lived through a tormented period of history similar to our own, who has diagnosed the ills of his times, and whose counsel could serve us today. There is, also, a great anxiety, easily discernible, in all this probing. Americans now seem to ask: What is this empire of ours which lives from alarm to alarm, which succeeds in doing its duty only in moments of great emotion and panic, whose goal seems to be only the conservation of material prosperity, the immobility of the line between cives and barbarians, and which is apparently ready to pay any sum in order not to be left alone with its fears? Is fear, now, the only force that moves us, when we never knew fear before? Americans seem to feel that, somewhere along the road, they have betrayed the spirit of their own past, and they want to find where the mistake was made, just as one goes back over a long list of figures to find the place where the sum went wrong.

Robert Hutchins said in 1933, "We have confused science with information, ideas with facts, knowledge with miscellaneous data. As the Renaissance could accuse the Middle Ages of being rich in principle and poor in facts, so we are entitled to inquire whether we are not rich in facts and poor in principles." What seemed to be in 1933 an interesting but technical problem for American college professors to debate when elaborating programs has suddenly become a tremendous question in which all of us and our descendants are interested.

Robert Hutchins spent many years at the University of Chicago changing the contents of American college education, experimenting with new courses, and trying to induce teachers to include more principles with the many facts. How successful has he been? How far did he go? It suddenly seemed extremely important (more important than interviewing statesmen) to assess how many of his ideas have remained with the students and teachers and, when I was in Chicago, I followed for a few days his favorite courses, the Humanities, in order to get an idea.

Boys and girls dressed in rough clothes, dungarees, and lumberjack shirts sat around large circular tables, listened, smoked, read and took notes as they debated texts which they had all read at home, largely complex fragments from an old philosopher. The teacher, who could be distinguished only by his age and by his less adventurous attire, sat at the same table, smoked and did not teach in the customary manner but merely acted as a Socratic chairman, prodding the debate with cautious questions, interrupting the flow of words to correct a false idea or to clarify a point, as if he wanted to avoid oppressing the students with his authority.

One morning we looked at the reproductions of Impressionist paintings; another morning we listened to records of a Beethoven quartet. The teacher would stop the turntable now and then to explain what was coming while the students followed the music on the score. "Pay attention now," he would say, "to the appearance, timid at first, then bolder, of this motif . . ." Once we earnestly debated for one hour the possibility, for man, to reach something like a metaphysical certainty.

It was all very civilized, pleasant, and familiar. There was the ugly girl with pimples who knew all the answers, the pretty girl who understood little and smiled but who was surrounded by four eager boys who showed her everything, turned the pages of her book and prompted her. There was the pale and bony boy who knew more than he was supposed to and tried to embarrass the teacher with curious analogies, parallels and deductions. Everything was seen not as a random piece of isolated information but as a sign of the times, island peaks emerging from the sea of history. And the conversation rambled agilely from one thing to another, Beethoven, Romanticism, Nationalism, Napoleon, the Hero, Carlyle, Democracy and Progress. The feeling came over me that I had seen all this before, in the *Liceo* in Italy in my youth, for instance, where teachers were few, taught three or four courses, Greek, philosophy, history, literature, forgot what hour they were in and jumped from one thing to another. Or café tables anywhere in Italy when I was very young and watched older men tossing revolutionary statements onto the marble tops like gamblers throwing down the winning card.

I had also heard the same sort of thing in the United States, years before, among young newspapermen, who debated Spengler over beer after work. This, however, was new: the recognition that talk was what young people needed, the round table, the cigarettes, the artificial informality. The school, in a fast-growing civilization, was apparently trying to do the job that, in other centuries or other countries, had been done by the family, the family books, the friends and the milieu. As gardeners cultivating tropical flowers in hothouses reproduce the soil, temperature and the moisture of the original place, the university was trying to grow ideas by surrounding them with the setting for polite conversation. It was a pleasant experiment. It would probably no more change American thinking habits than courses in refined cooking changed American ordinary cuisine.

One of the teachers told me, "We try to teach doubt. What the students get in every other course is certainty.

Everything is told to them as final, clear cut and definite. Here we want them to realize that everything is only a theory, a fragile construction, shaped by its time and other theories."

Mortimer Adler, I was told, was the man to see. He is the Erasmus of Chicago, the Moses leading a bewildered people to the promised land of immortal thoughts, the sage who almost alone battled against the philosophical heresies of the century. Adler had his office in an old house, included within the border of the campus of the University of Chicago. He did not teach, I was told, because he reserved all his time and all his energies to his enterprise, the publication of the Great Books and the compilation of the Syntopicon, his index of all the great ideas of Western man.

I found him an energetic young man dressed in tweeds for the outdoors and with a pipe clenched in his teeth. I had looked forward with some apprehension to a long and erudite conversation, to some speculation on the destiny of humanity or on the course of civilization.

Adler was too busy for that. The telephone rang almost continuously, and he talked with Pasadena, Boston, New York and Washington within a few minutes. His secretary continuously came in and out with papers. He was to leave a few hours later for California and had no time to waste. Every time I managed to advance a question, he handed me a printed extract from one of his works, magazine articles, lectures, or the publicity folders of his two projects. "You'll find an answer in there," he said.

I had time to scan the list of the Great Books while he was talking and noticed that many names were not there which I thought should be and that many names were included for reasons which escaped me. Why only *The Prince* by Machiavelli and not his commentaries on Livy, which really contain his thought? Why not de Tocqueville, Voltaire, and Lord Acton, to mention three at random? And why was Boswell included who was an imbecile whom the Anglo-Saxons love for reasons of their own? I asked Mr. Adler but he waved all objections aside.

"A committee has chosen the titles," he said, putting a hand on the telephone receiver. *"Errare humanum est. We're only men."*

Later he explained the point of the whole effort. Men who steeped themselves in great thoughts, who read the great authors without cuts and without notes, first hand, reached real maturity and could assume the responsibilities which democracy put on them. "Specialists," he said, "as we all tend to become, are adult in one little sector of human activity, their own, and children everywhere else. It is a dangerous situation, for the United States and for civilization."

He looked like a happy and busy man. He spoke as if he had no doubts that his Great Books and the Syntopicon (which looked somewhat like a telephone book to contact all thinkers of all centuries without wasting a minute) were to cure some of the ills of our age. More and more students, businessmen and ladies were taking on the Great Books. He himself was addressing a Great Books club in Chicago—when he had time. The thing was spreading east and west. Strangely enough, perhaps because his time was short and because he was handing me brightly colored literature describing his projects, and because he spoke in staccato and peremptory sentences between telephone calls, I could not think of him as a philosopher who could cure the ills of a materialistic age or who could remind contemporary Americans of their ancient civilization. He seemed rather like one more inventor who this time had found a rapid foolproof way to mature minds (as others had found a way to age whisky very quickly by means of temperature changes) or even like a promoter who develops the brain instead of the muscles.

I wondered whether Mr. Adler did not need a period of tranquillity in which to peruse some of his Great Books and acquire a little skepticism.

The word "skepticism" could probably be found easily in the Syntopicon.

I was tempted to conclude that morning in Chicago, listening to Mr. Mortimer Adler, that there was nothing startlingly new in what he had to say. The United

States was founded by men who had read the Great Books and who had chosen as an example the great republics of antiquity and a scholarly motto, *"E pluribus unum"* in Latin. For the last two centuries the poets, philosophers, and historians of antiquity have been studied uninterruptedly in the United States. Some universities pushed research in philology, European literatures, historical criticism, or philosophy sometimes beyond what had been done in Europe. On the other hand, there was something distinctly new. Mr. Adler may have sounded like other men selling commercial products or formulas to change the world overnight, but maybe that was only because of his manner. Still, what he was selling was genuine wisdom, the ancient authors, to a public who had recently developed a new and curious respect for the authority of dead men.

Twenty or more years ago when I studied in the United States, everybody more or less shared a youthful certainty that the world had been wrong through the centuries until that very morning and that the Americans were dispelling the fogs of obscurantism and were discovering a new system to beat life. The praise one sometimes read about a European author was that he wrote almost like an American, or, about an ancient writer, that he wrote like a modern. People studied the classics, but no special usefulness was attributed to their efforts. The old writers were to be read mainly as the witnesses of errors and superstitions which had retarded man's march in the past, or for the rare intuitions which had allowed them to glimpse at the truths which had become the commonplace of the modern age.

My teachers showed for Tacitus and Livy no more affection than Oriental language specialists for Indian or Chinese classics—documents worthy of serious study for many reasons but certainly not because they could teach us something about today. The present seemed beautiful but simply nothing compared to what the future would be. Day by day, readers of American newspapers were shown how the remnants of ancient barbarisms were doomed and gradually disappeared as the whole world slowly changed into an industrial paradise. Here an ancient kingdom had become a republic with a bicameral constitution, or an old craft had been superseded by machinery, there a dynamic leader had abolished the colorful costumes of the peasantry, or had razed a glorious city to the ground to build a modern one. Everywhere speed and uniformity were taking the place of outmoded ways of living.

That the anguish which grips America today could have something in common with what men in Athens, in Rome, in Byzantium, the Renaissance or the eighteenth century experienced, that maybe it is part and parcel of men's lot, that the ancient philosophers grappled with it and that the Doctors of the Church had something to say about it, is the discovery that many people in the United States are making. Not all, by any means, and not enough to change the outward aspects of life.

The man who started reading Thucydides or the Great Books has not abandoned his hope in scientific salvation and his expectation of future wonders. He is waiting now for the application of atomic energy to peaceful uses. Only this is true: the old contempt has been somehow transformed into cautious respect. Perhaps it was fear that taught many that they could not afford doing without the advice and help of dead men and foreigners. It may be the end of two isolationisms, space and time isolationisms. For some, the discovery has taken some joy out of living. A few, like Mr. Adler, have been tempted to think that this, now, was a better key to the universe, a new certainty. Others have experienced a feeling of liberation.

This I found important. Some Americans no longer feel they are the chosen people whose prosperity and salvation only matter, to whom God has entrusted the answer to the riddle. All of them are humbler. A few of them now believe they are people like other people. An old friend told me, "There may be an American way of life, an American know-how, an American approach to problems and American ideals, but there is no such thing as an American. Scratch the American and you find a human being." Travelers like me and many others and United States officials who explain their country to foreigners, we all make the same mistake—that of emphasizing those aspects of American life and past which are different because they make better reading.

At this point in history, what makes the United States a separate country, a permanent revolution, is becoming extremely unimportant. Our common future depends on how much America is Europe, how deeply her roots penetrate into our common civilization. G.I.'s fighting in Korea think they fight only for "freedom," one of the conquests of their forefathers. They also fight for Plato, Aristotle, Jesus Christ, Paul, Marcus Aurelius, the Doctors of the Church, medieval theologians, and thousands of others whom they have never heard of and Mr. Adler has forgot.

# VII

*Il y a aujourd'hui sur la terre deux grands peuples qui, partis de points différents, semblent s'avancer vers le même but: ce sont les Russes et les Américains. Tous deux ont grandi dans l'obscurité, et, tandis que les regards des hommes étaient occupés ailleurs, ils se sont placés tout à coup au premier rang des nations, et le monde a appris presque en même temps leur naissance et leur grandeur. Tous les autres peuples paraissent avoir atteint à peu près les limites qu'a tracées la nature, et n'avoir plus qu'a conserver; mais eux sont en croissance: tous les autres sont arrêtés ou n'avancent qu'avec mille efforts; eux seuls marchent d'un pas aisé et rapide dans une carrière dont l'œil ne saurait encore apercevoir la borne. L'Américain lutte contre les obstacles que lui oppose la nature. Le Russe est aux prises avec les hommes. L'un combat le désert et la barbarie; l'autre la civilization revêtue de toutes ses armes: aussi les conquêtes des Américains se font-elles avec le soc du laboureur, celles du Russe avec l'épée du soldat. Pour atteindre son but, le premier s'en repose sur l'intérêt personnel, et laisse agir sans les diriger la force et la raison des individus. Le second concentre en quelque sorte dans un homme toute la puissance de la société. L'un a pour principal moyen d'action la liberté, l'autre la servitude. Leur point de départ est différent, leurs voies sont diverses; néanmoins chacun d'eux semble appelé par un dessein secret de la Providence à tenir un jour dans ses mains les destinées de la moitié du monde.*      ALEXIS DE TOCQUEVILLE

*We are going to keep our temper. We are going to keep our strength.*      DWIGHT D. EISENHOWER

THE FUTURE OF ALL OF US depends on the decisions of both the Soviet Presidium and the United States government. Russian policy can be calculated exactly like the motions of the stars. The last few years have fully shown the Kremlin's persistent and uniform brutality, cynicism, and disregard for all civilized values. We have also learned that Soviet leaders follow, for opposite ideological reasons, the very same tactics which the Czarist ministers successfully adopted long ago, dictated no doubt by permanent factors and the national character. On June 4, 1853, one hundred years ago, *The Economist* printed the following valuation of Russian political habits, which with the change of a few names, could be applied to the present: "Now, menacing as is the aspect of the affairs in the East, we do not expect peace to be broken if Turkey is firm and if her allies are prompt, decisive, and united in their action, since it is the characteristic of Russian diplomacy to be as pliant as it is encroaching, and always to recede before a resolute front and an enterprise of doubtful and hazardous result. Russia never abandons a design, but is always ready to postpone it, if need be, till a more convenient season. She is as patient as she is pertinacious and will never risk her plum by endeavouring to gather it before it is ripe. The question, therefore, whether she will persist in her demands, will depend entirely on the nature and degree of the resistance she may meet with; the resistance will be measured by the unbending determination and bold attitude which the Sultan may display; and this again will in the main depend on the cordial and united aid which he may be authorized to rely on from France and England." In January, 1878, the mere presence of the British fleet cruising in the waters of Constantinople prevented a victorious Russian Army from conquering the defenseless city and the straits, which had been the goal of Czarist policy for centuries. In 1900, during the Boxer Rebellion, the Russian Far Eastern Army overran all Manchuria and retreated reluctantly after vigorous notes had been at last sent to St. Petersburg by the State Department and the Foreign Office. The troops surreptitiously returned a little later, as soon as the British and the Americans' backs were turned. Similarly in the face of the United States' firm decision to supply isolated Berlin at all costs, in 1948, the Soviets suddenly offered a *modus vivendi*. They also suggested a truce in Korea only after the United States forces had threatened the conquest of the whole peninsula to the Manchurian and Siberian borders. No fragile and unsubstantial obstacle ever stops the Russians; they are shrewd enough to disregard moral appeals, noble speeches, injunctions, insults, prayers, and

Platonic declarations of theoretical aims. Not even the threatened use of armed forces is enough, unless they are strong enough, commanded firmly, and ready to fight, come what may.

United States foreign policy, on the other hand, looks to observers abroad, including the Russians, unpredictable, erratic, contradictory, and unreliable.

Three roads are now open to the United States:

—war with Russia or China or both, now or in the near future;

—submission to the Kremlin's will;

—armed patience.

For war to break out it is not necessary that the Joint Chiefs of Staff, the President, or the Cabinet set a definite date for the guns to start shooting. It is enough that, at a certain moment, when rising armaments give the American government enough confidence, when circumstances are favorable, the patience of the State Department should wear thin in the face of new provocations, the answers to communist advances become more humiliating, American demands more peremptory, and requests for the Soviets' unconditional surrender more intransigent.

Similarly, submission to the Kremlin's will, which would just as surely lead to war, may be masked once again as the honest desire for peace, reasonable acceptance of reality, blind trust in woolly international bodies and collective security, all this too easily decorated by journalists and politicians with noble and pathetic rhetoric.

The first two roads are, of course, the most natural for Americans to choose. They both satisfy deep and ancient urges in the national character. The first appeals to the Americans' traditional jealousy of their force and dignity, their wish to resist all blackmail ("Millions for defence but not one cent for tribute") and to face all challenges with courage and determination. The second appeals to the Americans' perennial quest for the earthly paradise in which all men will be brothers and think of nothing but the production and consumption of vast quantities of consumers' goods. Is that not the perfect state, dreamed of by the Founding Fathers, which is the ultimate and inevitable goal that all men, including the Soviet Russians, long for and must eventually reach? Is it not then a dangerous folly to retard the advent of the millennium by clinging to outmoded fears and precautions?

The third road is the only one which may insure peace. Have the Americans the moral strength, the wisdom, and the staying power to keep to armed patience? It is not easy to determine. It is the course most difficult to their *volksgeist*. Their nation has been founded and populated by the impatient of all the world, fretting at obsolete systems, rules, hierarchies and dogmas, who were not stopped by nature's hostility and the disadvantages of physical laws. It must be admitted, too, that until now impatience has paid fabulous dividends and any reluctance to abandon it as the supreme virtue can easily be understood. Yet abandon it they must, if catastrophe is to be avoided. Mature Americans are resignedly aware of the necessity. President Eisenhower himself voiced the warning. "There is going to be no Munich," he said, "and at the same time there is going to be no risk of a general war . . . We're going to keep our temper. We're going to build our strength . . . But remember that in these vast problems that affect the lives of every one of us there is no thought that you can cut the knots. You must untie them, slowly and laboriously."

These words had a strange and hopeful sound coming from the leader of a people who have been traditionally hacking away at all kinds of knots for the last century and a half.

It is difficult to determine which road the United States will eventually take because a large number of authoritative Americans seem to be advocating all three possible courses with a seductive wealth of arguments. Furthermore, a fourth and confusing group, which includes some of the more eminent political and military leaders, is in favor of a fourth and impossible choice, the most dangerous: "Disarmed impatience." It combines the two most tempting features, the economies of appeasement and the pleasures of overbearing intransigence. These men apparently want withdrawal from Europe, vast economies in the armed forces budget, a reduction of foreign aid, the erection of a *Festung*

*Amerika* to defend and isolate the national way of life from the discomforts of history, and, at the same time, to grasp the initiative from the Russians' hands, to adopt an increasingly stiff attitude towards their wiles, to reject all possible compromises, and all this with as few allies as possible.

Which road will the United States eventually take?

Those traditional virtues which have helped make the United States the richest and most powerful nation of all times, have won two world wars, and have saved the peace, are no longer enough, just as the simple optimism of past generations is not a sufficient guide to the complex life of today. This is the American crisis, the discovery that their philosophy is inadequate and sometimes misleading. People are visibly trying everywhere, in all fields, to find an answer. Some go back over the road their ancestors traveled, to discover which was the wrong turn they took. Some religiously cling to the ancient habits and to a provincial outlook. Some earnestly study the Great Books in search of the ancient wisdom, having understood that, in matters relating to man, the old answers are the best answers. Some, like Thomas Merton and the converts to Catholicism, look for certainty in prayer and the teachings of the Doctors of the Church. Many want to forget the rest of the world, with all its problems, forget history and its lessons, as if the Americans were a race apart and the United States another planet, and live empirically day by day, relying on the national capacity to face emergencies. All this (which we have tried to discover in the

United States) is reflected in private behavior and in politics, in the confused struggles between the various tendencies, and in the contradictory pronouncements from Washington.

The spectacle of the American crisis cannot help provoke serious repercussions abroad. Foreigners never know how much authority American leaders really have, what pledges will be kept, what Congress will do to treaties, promises, and agreed plans of action, and how soon public opinion will tire of a specific line.

All problems seem to be seen and solved separately, as if they were isolated, with no relation one with the others. United States officials diligently see to it that no Western nation exchange vital goods with the communist world; Congressmen make it as difficult as possible for the same nations to sell their best and cheapest products to the United States; at the same time, economic missions in those very same nations use all known technical and psychological means to boost the production of goods which cannot be all consumed internally and cannot be sold abroad except with the greatest difficulties. American agricultural lobbyists are frantically trying to find a way to export grains and cotton abroad, to save the farmers' purchasing power and to stop the fall of prices, while European nations expensively try to raise all they need at home or buy it at higher prices from other countries than the United States, because they have no dollars and cannot earn enough.

Clement Attlee tried to express the doubts of bewildered Europeans in the House of Commons. He said,

"The Administration might desire to spend many millions on support, whether of armaments or some other project, but Congress might cut down the sum by several millions of dollars. The Administration might wish to encourage our exports to the United States but, as in the case of Chief Joseph Dam, influences frustrate the Administration's policy. The government of the United States is not really master in its own house. It was found on occasion that there was one policy run by the Treasury, another by the State Department, and perhaps another by the Pentagon."

Naturally confusion is the price one sometimes has to pay for liberty. From confusion, debates, and contradictions come the only decisions which a people will wholeheartedly obey. They are the defects of all democracies. No government is really master in its own house, not even one of Clement Attlee's, and can never accomplish all it intends to do unhindered by particular interests and strong opposition. France's political coherence and continuity are less dependable than the United States'. Also within the Soviet Presidium are forces working against each other and one never knows which one will win in the end. It may be proved that there often is one policy run by the Foreign Office, one by the B.B.C., one by the British Army, one by the Intelligence Service, and perhaps another by the Board of Trade. Historians can also point to periods in the past when the contradictions in the American system were even more flagrant than now, periods when the struggle between President, public opinion, special interests, and

Congress was more paralyzing than it is now. Why is it that what appears natural, inevitable, amusing, or merely deplorable in other countries or in the past seems ominously dangerous now and in the United States?

The answer is, of course, that never in history has the destiny of so many people, practically of the whole born and unborn human race, depended on the decision of so few men. It is America's job to provide leadership, to maintain peace, to facilitate economic exchanges, to further prosperity. Whether she likes it or not, whether she acknowledges it or refuses to face the fact, all her decisions, even the small, insignificant and private ones, have world-wide repercussions. She is the economic, military and political heart of the world. As she goes, so go the rest of us. All problems are hers, as past problems were in the hands of the Romans and the English, because, if a situation deteriorates and war breaks out, her soldiers will die in that war and her money will finance it. The European dollar gap, French instability, German desire for unity, the Italian unemployed, Japanese lack of raw materials and markets, nationalism in the Near East, revolt in Africa, all these and many more are as American as the Negro problem in the South, communist infiltration in the civil service or soil erosion. All these problems and many more are influenced by decisions taken in Washington, or by the lack of decision, or by decisions taken absent-mindedly without thought to consequences. Even the decision to forget the rest of the world and to go back to a peaceful, provincial life would provoke immediate chaos, just as the decision in the twenties and thirties to sell more than to buy abroad filled Fort Knox with gold and helped drive the world toward war. Naturally, nobody expects the United States to solve all the world's problems. But she must worry about them, be conscious of their existence, and do the best she can. She can no longer afford to ignore them.

The United States has done a great job until now, but the forces which have sustained her have mostly been fear and moral indignation, emotions which tend to run out of control. Her ability was purely empirical, dictated by circumstances, modified by newspaper headlines and moods, without well-founded and constant rules, and therefore her policy was mostly defensive (as policies always are when designed on the spur of the moment to face an outside threat), weak, and too expensive, both for her and for her allies. As the United States cannot do everything—pay for every weapon, shoot every gun, build and fly every plane, contribute all the casualties—from now on, she must devise some means by which others will be encouraged to carry their share of the burden. To do that Americans must first of all understand foreigners, realize they are not other Americans, know what makes them tick and what makes them die willingly. The United States must establish a smooth-running system, which will allow the free world to earn their keep and spare enough money for the necessary armaments, fixed long-range plans which will not be disturbed by a vote or a speech, policies which will appeal to all the allies. Apparently the defense of

the American way of life, as an international ideal, is
not strong enough for people who have never tried it,
have seen it only in the cinema, and will never afford it.

The whole Western world is wary of the United
States. Statesmen are reluctant to risk their own, their
parties', and their governments' future, on something
they do not quite understand, the American mind, Constitution, optimistic ideals and future intentions. Years
ago, at the outset of the Marshall Plan, the Italian government was officially scolded for having salted away,
in the form of gold bullion, dollars which were intended for the purchase of specified raw materials. The
ministers, like careful fathers and good farmers, had
deemed it wise to think of leaner days to come when
the unexpected rainfall of dollars would cease as mysteriously as it had started. That is the natural reaction to
all American policies: everybody tries to hedge his bets,
not be caught off balance by any sudden shifts. Everybody is frightened by the repeated and unnecessary
announcements of elevated ethical ideals which are supposed to inspire all of us. France wants a deal in Indo-
China and wants to prevent Germany from rearming.
She does not trust American guarantees for her future
safety. Sir Winston Churchill wants to deal directly with
Malenkov, wants to keep as good relations as possible
with the communist world, trade flowing across the
Iron Curtain, diplomatic channels open. The whole free
world is preparing for the day when the United States
will no longer carry her present enormous burden, without having been able to devise a more stable and eco-

nomical structure. The day may never come, of course, but a statesman's duty is to make ready for it.

This, in conclusion, is the turning point. Nothing is lost yet. The Atlantic alliance is still a strong union of nations with a common will and a common policy. The Soviets are biding their time. The new Kremlin leaders are waiting for a better day, while keeping their armed forces in readiness for the moment of weakness and dissension in the free camp which Stalin foresaw. Can the Americans make the shift from the psychology of emergency, which is what their historical experience has taught them, to the psychology of the long pull? Can they accept the difficult policy of "armed patience"? By the ironic law which governs all human affairs, the more they are resigned to seeing their cities razed by atomic attacks, their youth massacred, their civilian population decimated, the less will the probabilities be of all these things happening. The decision belongs with the United States.

George Kennan wrote what all mature Americans know:

"The issue is in essence a test of the over-all worth of the United States as a nation among nations. Surely there never was a fairer test of national quality than this. In the light of these circumstances, the thoughtful observer will find no cause of complaint in the Kremlin's challenge to American society. He will rather experience a certain gratitude to Providence which, by providing the American people with this implacable challenge, has made their entire security as a nation dependent on their pulling themselves together and accepting the responsibilities of moral and political leadership that history plainly intended them to bear."

Peace is entrusted to the youthfulness of the United States, a new nation ready for sacrifices and bold experiments to bring about the improbable but desirable world of tomorrow. Above all, we think, peace is entrusted to the venerable antiquity of the United States—as ancient as any European country—which is again discovering the old rules of life—as old as man—which are part of its inheritance as well as of our own.